Praise for The Resilience Wor

"It's hard to be a kid today. Kids see more, know more, and do more today than ever before but some of what they see are bad examples, some of what they know is challenging to everyone, and some of what they do are what those bad examples encourage. This book is a practice field for good, showing children in a step-by-step way how to develop the flexible strength needed to prosper. If you love children, you will love the support for healthy growth this book provides. Highly recommended."

—**Steven C. Hayes, PhD**, Nevada Foundation Professor of psychology at the University of Nevada, Reno; and originator and codeveloper of acceptance and commitment therapy (ACT)

"This urgently needed workbook brilliantly engages young people to build their resilience skill sets. They'll be better prepared to handle life's curveballs *and* to get the most out of life in joyful times. I love that this work honors emotions and teaches kids how to own them, process them, and even celebrate that they have them. Critically, *The Resilience Workbook for Kids* will also prepare you to be the kind of adult who can nurture young people in their resilience journey. I genuinely believe this wonderful tool kit will change lives!"

—**Kenneth R. Ginsburg, MD, MS, Ed**, coauthor of *Building Resilience in Children and Teens*, and director of the Center for Parent and Teen Communication at www.parentandteen.com

"Resilience is more than a buzzword. It's a critical component of our health and wellness because it allows us to weather and withstand life's challenges big and small. *The Resilience Workbook for Kids* is a beautifully written, inclusive, engaging, fun, work-as-you-go guide with relevant and sensitive examples that will help kids understand resilience and strengthen it within them. A timely must-read for kids, teens, and the adults who mentor, teach, and love them."

—**Julie Lythcott-Haims**, New York Times bestselling author of *How to Raise an Adult*

"Caren Baruch-Feldman and Rebecca Comizio have written a wonderful, science-based guide to help children manage their emotions and enhance their resilience. Authoritative, comprehensive, and accessible, *The Resilience Workbook for Kids* is a gift."

—**Ethan Kross, PhD**, director of the Self-Control and Emotion Laboratory, and professor of psychology at the University of Michigan; professor of management and organizations at Ross School of Business; and author of *Chatter*

"How do we help children build resilience? By giving them *The Resilience Workbook for Kids*! This brilliant guide is professional and practical, timely and timeless, warm and wise. Children need to build their resilience muscles; Caren Baruch-Feldman and Rebecca Comizio have written the book that will serve as the perfect gym."

—**Lisa Damour, PhD**, author of *Untangled* and *Under Pressure*

"A fitness routine for emotions. A guide to beating stress. A road map to mental wellness. *The Resilience Workbook for Kids* is all of this wrapped into an exciting and engaging tool kit for young people facing emotional challenges. From introducing and teaching the science of resilience, all the way to practice and habit building, this book is a total wellness package."

—**Renee Jain**, *New York Times* bestselling coauthor of *Superpowered*, and founder of GoZen!

"This terrific workbook is filled with tips and techniques to help kids develop their resilience. The activities and reflections allow kids to be deeply involved in learning about themselves in a fun way. This is an invaluable resource for parents, teachers and counselors."

—**Lea Waters, PhD**, author of *The Strength Switch*

"*The Resilience Workbook for Kids* is filled with tons of rich ideas and creative strategies to help children develop resilience. The ideas are presented in ways that will work both for children and for the adults who work with them. The graphics, puzzles, and interactive features are quite attractive and make pursuing resilience fun. I heartily recommend this book to educators, caregivers, and kids!"

—**Thomas R. Hoerr, PhD**, scholar in residence at UM-St. Louis, and author of many SEL books, including *The Formative Five*

"This book is a much-needed guide to help children navigate the world today. A highly creative, engaging, and enjoyable book for children, and one that can help all kids build their resilience."

—**Scott Barry Kaufman, PhD**, humanistic psychologist; author of *Transcend*, *Wired to Create*, and *Ungifted*; and host of the *Psychology Podcast*

The Resilience Workbook for Kids

Fun CBT Activities to Help You Bounce Back from Stress and Grow from Challenges

Caren Baruch-Feldman, PhD • Rebecca Comizio, MA, MEd

Instant Help Books
An Imprint of New Harbinger Publications, Inc.

Publisher's Note

This publication is designed to provide accurate and authoritative information in regard to the subject matter covered. It is sold with the understanding that the publisher is not engaged in rendering psychological, financial, legal, or other professional services. If expert assistance or counseling is needed, the services of a competent professional should be sought.

INSTANT HELP, the Clock Logo, and NEW HARBINGER are trademarks of New Harbinger Publications, Inc.

NCEO MEMBER

Distributed in Canada by Raincoast Books

Instant Help Books
An imprint of New Harbinger Publications, Inc.
5674 Shattuck Avenue
Oakland, CA 94609
www.newharbinger.com

The resilience survey in activity 1 of the "Parents and Professionals" supplement is adapted from THE RESILIENCE WORKBOOK by Glenn Schiraldi, copyright © 2017 by Glenn Schiraldi/New Harbinger Publications. Used by permission of New Harbinger Publications.

The activity "Self-Compassion Break" in the "Bonus Activities and Worksheets" supplement is adapted from THE MINDFUL SELF-COMPASSION WORKBOOK by Kristen Neff and Christopher Germer, copyright © 2018 by Kristen Neff and Christopher Germer/Guilford Press. Used by permission of Guilford Press.

Cover design and illustration by Sara Christian. Interior book design by Amy Shoup. Interior illustrations by Valeria Chipao. Acquired by Elizabeth Hollis Hansen.
Edited by Gretel Hakanson

MIX
Paper from responsible sources
FSC® C011935

Library of Congress Cataloging-in-Publication Data on file

Printed in the United States of America

25 24 23

10 9 8 7 6 5 4 3

She stood in the storm, and when the wind did not blow her way, she adjusted her sails.

—Elizabeth Edwards

This book is dedicated to my mother, father, husband, and children. Dad, I miss you. I know if you were here, you'd have loved the boat analogies. Thank you all, for your love and support. You have made me who I am.

—Caren

This book is dedicated to my father, the man who taught me to always look at the bright side, be grateful for the little things, and keep working hard. Thanks, Dad, for giving me the best example of resilience a kid could've had, and for looking out for your grandkids from where you are.

—Rebecca

Contents

PART 3: Creating Resilient Thinking

PART 4: Resilient Actions: Ready, Set, Go!

PART 5: Building Resilience All Around You

Foreword

Since I began my career in clinical psychology many years ago, I have witnessed several major changes of focus that have had a direct impact on my work. One of the most salient was a shift from a "medical model," with an emphasis on identifying and "fixing deficits," to a strength-based perspective that assumed, as a primary goal, recognizing, honoring, and harnessing each person's strengths, or what I have referred to since the early 1980s as their "islands of competence."

This shift is associated with the emergence of the "positive psychology" field and an increased interest in defining individual and environmental forces that contribute to our ability to cope more effectively with stress and challenges, to thrive in the face of adversity, and to become more resilient. In my writings, especially with my colleague Dr. Sam Goldstein, we emphasize that specifying what is "wrong" with a person may yield information about that person's current life but that nurturing the strengths of that person in different domains will be much more pertinent to what they can accomplish in life.

This belief prompted me as a clinician, consultant, and parent to pose the following question: How do resilient children and adults see themselves and the world differently from those who are not resilient? This represented more than an academic question. It was my position that the more precisely we could delineate factors associated with resilience, the more we could implement effective strategies to reinforce resilience in our children as well as in ourselves.

As I began to share ideas with parents, teachers, mental health clinicians, and other caregivers about what actions they might initiate to nurture a resilient mindset and behaviors in children and adolescents, I was frequently asked, "Are there programs or exercises and activities that kids can use by themselves or with the assistance of adults to help them to be more confident problem solvers and more resilient?"

In answering that question, I can reply that we now have available a wonderful resource authored by Dr. Caren Baruch-Feldman and Rebecca Comizio to assist us in fostering a resilient outlook and behaviors in children. *The Resilience Workbook for Kids* is a veritable treasure chest of ideas, strategies, and engaging activities that can be used by children alone or with the input of adults.

Caren and Rebecca introduce themselves as captains guiding kids and their caregivers to navigate challenging seas on the journey toward resilience. They perform this role with impressive skill as they describe concepts such as resilience, personal control, stress, problem solving, and coping strategies in ways that are understandable and usable by children and early teens. As captains, they constantly engage the reader in a variety of activities that are relevant and fun and facilitate learning that can be used for one's entire life. In addition, parents, therapists, and other caregivers will discover that when they are involved with the exercises and activities described in this workbook, their role and responsibilities are well-defined, ensuring greater success in interacting with their children.

Augmenting the richness of Caren and Rebecca's work are additional online activities. One group of these activities is based on the concept of self-compassion; the activities involve ways to take care of and be kind to oneself. The other two main sets of activities found online are rich in information and strategies. One is geared for teachers and other school personnel, while the second is for parents and professionals outside of education. These activities focus on practical ideas for us as adults to nurture our own resilience, and they also highlight realistic, innovative interventions for enhancing the lives of our children and students.

Caren and Rebecca are to be commended for creating a workbook that will be valued by all who have the privilege of raising, educating, and working with children and nurturing those attributes associated with hope and resilience. It is a wonderful gift we provide for the next generation.

—Robert Brooks, PhD
Faculty, Harvard Medical School (part time)
Coauthor, *Raising Resilient Children* and *Tenacity in Children*

A Letter to Parents and Professionals

Welcome! We are so glad you have chosen *The Resilience Workbook for Kids*. In this book, you'll find science, strategies, and a whole toolkit of exercises to help children cope with stress, navigate adversity, and grow through challenges. Children need this support now more than ever! Living in a world of uncertainty, with significant political and socioeconomic unrest, twenty-four-hour news cycles, and physical and environmental health risks (including the COVID-19 pandemic), makes emotional agility, adaptability, and a growth mindset essential skills for children to develop.

The good news is that resilience can be taught. Resilience isn't a trait but a set of skills that allows people not only to survive challenges and difficult times but to flourish during and after them. Like any other type of learning, these skills can be broken down and then practiced.

In each activity, children will learn about a skill and why it's important ("Learn It"), have an opportunity to practice the skill ("Do It"), and then have time to strengthen the skill ("Strengthen It"). Surveys, real-life examples, and games are provided throughout the book to reinforce learning and make the material engaging and fun. We have also included bonus activities throughout the workbook for children to complete with a special adult. These exercises are intended to help parents, caregivers, and professionals build a positive relationship with children—a key factor in building resilience.

Before you introduce this workbook to a child, please visit http://www.newharbinger.com/49166 and download the section titled "Adults: Put Your Oxygen Mask on First." Just like flight attendants instruct adult passengers to put on their oxygen masks first, it's important for you to learn how to cope with stress and deal with setbacks in your own life before you help a child build these skills. In doing these online activities, you'll be able to assess how resilient you are now, learn ways to grow your own resilience, and discover how best to support a child's development of resilience skills.

Once you have completed the downloaded activities, you will be ready to guide the child you care for or work with through the activities in this workbook.

In part 1, children will learn what resilience is and why it's important. They will understand the difference between helpful and unhelpful stress and the impact that toxic stress can have on their minds and bodies.

In part 2, children will find ways to make emotions their friends. They will discover ways to increase positive emotions and that all emotions have value. They will also acquire techniques to *actively respond* to events rather than *automatically react* when feeling overwhelmed.

In part 3, children will uncover their unhelpful thinking traps, challenge negative beliefs, and build optimism and a growth mindset. They will identify their core values, increase their capacity for hope, and learn to see challenges as opportunities for growth.

In part 4, children will turn those thoughts into actions by developing strategies that strengthen competence, flexibility, and self-care. They'll learn to problem solve, be brave, and cope with difficulties, using their strengths and their ability to advocate for themselves as best they can.

In part 5, children will discover that resilience does not exist only in them; it's equally important to grow resilience by gaining support from others. Furthermore, culture, context, and environment play essential roles in building a child's resilience. So, in this section, kids will practice activities that encourage them to connect with others, act in ways that benefit others, and gain a sense of purpose.

The Resilience Workbook for Kids is based on the latest research, cognitive behavioral therapy (CBT) techniques, and positive psychology strategies while still remaining fun and engaging for children. (The references for the book, which show the research the activities are based on, can be downloaded from http://www.newharbinger.com/49166.)

Younger children or beginning readers may need support from you or another adult as they complete the activities. But no matter how the children you know work through *The Resilience Workbook for Kids*, they will gain valuable skills that will increase their confidence, flexibility, and resilience.

Thank you for your willingness to take this journey and for being a "charismatic adult" in a child's life—an adult from whom a child gathers strength and support.

Warmest wishes,

Caren Baruch-Feldman and Rebecca Comizio

P.S. If you are an educator or a school professional, check out the additional guide we've written to help you increase the resilience of the students in your school. It's available for you to download at http://www.newharbinger.com/49166. At the same site, you'll also find some fun posters for three core interventions in this book—the STORMS approach to building resilience, the strategy of "accepting the yuck" (activity 8), and the strategy of "pumping up the positive" (activity 9)—that you can hang up in your classroom to remind yourself and your students of these fundamentals of building resilience.

P.P.S. Don't forget, all adults, please visit http://www.newharbinger.com/49166 and download the section titled "Adults: Put Your Oxygen Mask on First" to complete the activities there—because resilience in children starts with the grown-ups who care for them.

A Letter to Kids

Hello, friend! Welcome to *The Resilience Workbook for Kids*. Do you know what resilience is? Resilience is the ability to cope with life's ups and downs and deal with challenges—sometimes to even grow stronger from them. By "challenges," we mean big things like serious health problems, a divorce in your family, and the pandemic. We also mean things that are not as big, but still tough, like not making a team or arguing with a friend. All these challenges are hard to go through and can make you feel scared, angry, or frustrated. But you can learn to handle them if you develop resilience.

Being resilient doesn't mean you don't have setbacks or big emotions. It does mean that you face these obstacles head-on and with a positive attitude. Resilient people know that the mad, bad, or sad things we all go through don't last forever. They also know that these things happen to all people, not just them. Having this knowledge helps people cope better with the hard things they're facing.

There are five parts in this book. Each has activities that focus on a different piece of resilience. In each activity, you'll learn about a topic ("Learn It"), have an opportunity to practice the skill you're learning ("Do It"), and then strengthen the skill ("Strengthen It").

As you work through the parts, you'll learn things like what stress is and how it can be helpful or not. You'll also learn the role that your emotions and thoughts play in helping you deal with stress. And you'll learn how to be brave, solve problems, and take care of yourself. You'll also learn why it's important to have support people around you to help you get through challenging times. Each part of the book will end with a puzzle, as a fun way to check your knowledge. We know the puzzles can be hard. They also build resilience! Just like most things that require resilience, getting support can be helpful. So, remember you can always ask an adult for help if you need it.

You should know that both of us have been on our own resilience journeys. Rebecca is a first-generation American. Her parents were both born in India, and she grew up in a town with no other families of color. She often felt lonely and like she didn't belong. Her mother also had a serious mental illness that made it hard for her to take care of Rebecca and her little sister. But Rebecca's father taught her about resilience because he never gave up on his children or his American dream. Eventually, after many setbacks, he became successful. Her and her father's experiences inspired Rebecca to become a therapist so she could help other kids who are going through hard things.

Caren also experienced the need to be resilient. A few years ago, after working very hard and achieving some great career and health goals, she started to feel ill. She went from doctor to doctor, but no one could figure out what was wrong. Eventually, she learned her body was producing too much of the stress hormone cortisol. She needed surgery to fix it. Her recovery was long. But Caren got support from her family and friends. She also reminded herself that this was just a moment in time and to focus on what she could control. Slowly, her body started to heal, and she felt better. She still deals with headaches from time to time, but through this experience, she built her resilience.

Our goal with this book is to help *you* navigate your own stormy seas. We'll be your captains, helping you develop the skills to ride the waves and manage the storms. We'll teach you the STORMS approach to building resilience.

STORMS stands for:

S. Starts with adult resilience. When adults grow their own resilience, they can manage their own stress and better help you.

T. Teach yourself the skills and science of resilience.

O. Own all your emotions so they don't control you. Feel your feelings, even the hard ones.

R. Rule your mind so you can think happier and more helpful thoughts.

M. Manage your behaviors so you can cope more and stress less.

S. Seek a support network (parent, teacher, friend, neighbor) so you have someone there to always help you.

Before you dive into the book, take a moment to imagine yourself on a boat out at sea in the middle of a big storm. The boat is bobbing up and down, the waves are crashing, and land is nowhere in sight. Now imagine that you are on this same boat with an experienced captain, and you have strong swimming skills, a life jacket, an anchor, a map, and the North Star to guide you. Do you think you will do better in this storm? We do! If you follow the STORMS steps, you will have everything you need to turn stress into bravery, confidence, and in a word, "resilience." Are you ready to take this voyage with us? We can't wait for you to start. Welcome aboard!

Fondly,

Your captains,

Caren and Rebecca

PART 1

Understanding Resilience

"Life is not about how fast you run or how high you climb but how well you bounce."

—Tigger from Winnie the Pooh

WHAT YOU'LL DISCOVER

Welcome! We are delighted that you are starting this journey with us. In this part, you will learn about the science of resilience.

In part 1, you will learn:

- What resilience is
- Why it's important
- How much you have
- What stress is
- That some stress is good for you, and some stress can actually make you sick, if you don't have good ways to deal with it

ACTIVITY 1

What Is Resilience?

LEARN IT

What is resilience? Not sure? That's okay! Scientists define "resilience" as the ability to cope with life's ups and downs. Sometimes it makes you even stronger than you were before.

Being resilient means coping with big things, like health problems or getting hurt. It also means dealing with everyday setbacks (though we know those don't feel small!), like not getting along with a friend or doing poorly on a test.

When you're resilient, you learn from past challenges so you can face future obstacles with greater confidence and strength.

Being resilient doesn't mean you don't have strong emotions or challenges. But it means that you face setbacks and big emotions head-on and with hope so you can come back at least as strong as before—or even stronger. Resilient people don't let mad, bad, or sad things take over. They find ways to make different choices, begin to feel better, and keep moving toward their goals.

You might not think of yourself as a resilient person. But resilience isn't all-or-nothing, something you either have or don't have. Most people are resilient in some areas and not resilient yet in others. No matter how resilient you are now or how overwhelming some events may be, resilience is something you can get better at.

We're excited to show you how you can learn to be more resilient. Let's get started.

DO IT

Below is a list of scenarios that young people like you are facing. For each scenario, if the kid is acting in ways that are resilient—if they are coping and finding ways to grow—circle **RESILIENT**. If they're still struggling, circle **Not There YET**.

1. Mateo found out he didn't make the soccer team, and he's super disappointed. His mother gives him a hug and reminds him that his older brother didn't make the team the first time he tried out. Mateo feels better when he remembers he can try out again in the spring after some more practice.

   RESILIENT **Not There YET**

2. Christopher is struggling with his online classes. He finds the classes boring and hates looking at himself online. He shuts the camera off and decides to text his friends.

   RESILIENT **Not There YET**

3. Maria's mother just told her that she lost her job and that they need to move to another town. Maria is worried about the move. She asks her mom if she can come along to look at new apartments. She's still not sure she wants to move, but she knows she and her mom will figure this out together.

   RESILIENT **Not There YET**

4. Thea feels overwhelmed with her schoolwork. There's just too much of it—and she doesn't understand any of the directions. She decides she'll do her work tomorrow. When her mom asks her how she is doing with her work, she says, "I did it" (even though she hasn't). She feels bad about

lying, but she doesn't know how to get out of this mess. She is hoping her mom doesn't learn the truth.

RESILIENT **Not There YET**

5. Carl feels sad and lonely since his dad left. He misses his dad but feels guilty about missing him because his dad would drink, get angry, and hurt his mother. Carl decides to talk to the school psychologist about his confusing feelings.

RESILIENT **Not There YET**

How was that—easy or hard? Here are answers to the questions, with explanations.

1. Mateo is **RESILIENT** about not making the team. He is disappointed about not making the team and works through his feelings by getting support from his mother. He also thinks optimistically about the situation.

2. Christopher is **Not There YET** with his resilience. He is feeling overwhelmed, which is understandable, but is avoiding the situation instead of finding ways to cope.

3. Maria is **RESILIENT**. Understandably, she has strong feelings about the news, but she shows resilience by getting support and focusing on what she can control.

4. Thea is **Not There YET** with her resilience. Like Christopher, she is avoiding instead of facing the challenge.

5. Carl is **RESILIENT**. His family situation is painful, but by reaching out to the school psychologist and talking about his feelings, he is taking the first steps to help himself cope with a difficult and confusing situation.

In summary, it's what Mateo, Maria, and Carl *do* and the *support* they receive that helps them be more resilient than Christopher and Thea.

STRENGTHEN IT

If you were Christopher's friend and you wanted to help him deal with his online classes, what would you say to him? Try writing a letter to Christopher with some advice.

Need help? We wrote a letter to Thea, who's also struggling, that can help you write your letter to Christopher.

> Dear Thea,
>
> We know you feel overwhelmed with your schoolwork. When kids aren't certain how to do their schoolwork, it's good to ask for help. No one will think you aren't smart if you need help. Let your mom know the truth. She's on your side!

Do you see in our example how we tried to help Thea? First, we validated her feelings. This means we let her know how it's understandable that she is feeling overwhelmed about all that work. Next, we shared with her that no one would look down on her for asking for help. We also reminded her that her mom is on her team.

Now you try.

Dear Christopher,

____

____

____

____

____

____

One way to help yourself when you are struggling is to write down your own thoughts and feelings as if you were writing to a dear friend. The next time you're going through something hard, think about what you told Christopher. See if you can tell yourself the same sorts of things.

Don't worry if you feel that you're more like Thea and Christopher than Mateo, Maria, and Carl. You're just beginning your resilience voyage, and you're just not there YET!

ACTIVITY 2

How Resilient Are You?

LEARN IT

Now that you know a little more about what it means to be resilient, let's get started by thinking about how resilient you already are when you are facing stressful situations. Answer the prompts in the survey honestly. There are no wrong answers. This is just an opportunity for you to learn about your strengths and the areas you may need to grow.

At the end of the book, you will retake the survey. We are optimistic that your ability to handle stressful situations and come back from them will grow.

DO IT

For each of the prompts in the "Resilience Checkup" below, circle the thumbs-up for "frequently," the thumbs-sideways for "sometimes," and the thumbs-down for "rarely."

Resilience Checkup

	Frequently	Sometimes	Rarely
During difficult times, I keep calm and think about what could help.			
I am flexible. If my usual way of doing things isn't working, I try something else.			
I learn important lessons from my mistakes and from what other people do and go through.			
I'm good at solving problems. I can think logically, be creative, or use common sense.			
When I feel stressed, I have trusted adults I can talk to.			
I can find something funny even in tough situations, and I can laugh at myself.			
I can learn and grow from challenging experiences.			

STRENGTHEN IT

So, how did you do? Did you have mostly thumbs-up, thumbs-down, or thumbs-sideways? Which one did you circle the most?

If you had mostly thumbs-ups, you're doing well. If you had more thumbs-downs or sideways, you're still doing well! The best thing about this questionnaire is that there are no wrong responses. It's just about finding out where you are now: what your strengths are, and where you might be able to grow. As long as you thought about and answered each question honestly, you get a score of 100 percent, or an A+! The more you think about and understand yourself and the stresses you might be facing, the more confident and resilient you will become.

ACTIVITY 3

Why Resilience Matters

LEARN IT

You may be wondering, *Why is resilience so important? Why do I need this?* The answer is that when you have greater resilience, you feel more capable, confident, and proud of yourself after managing hard things. Scientists have discovered that when kids are more resilient, they are better at understanding and talking about their feelings. They also do better in school, and they have better relationships with friends and grown-ups.

If that's not enough to convince you, the fact is everyone will face challenges throughout their lives. It's possible that you might be going through something stressful right now. That's why learning to work through challenges is not only necessary, but doing it intentionally offers a powerful opportunity for you to get stronger. Doesn't that sound good?

DO IT

Below are examples of resilient people from all walks of life. Through their life stories, we can learn what true resilience is and why it's essential. Try to match each resilient person with their story.

Malala Yousafzai	**A.** This competitive surfer lost her arm in a shark attack when she was only thirteen. That event led her to be in the public spotlight, from talk shows to a Hollywood movie based on her life. Not only did she return to the water, but she went on to ride some of the world's biggest waves.
Michael Jordan	**B.** Despite danger, this schoolgirl spoke out against banning girls from getting an education. She spoke up against the government and then was shot. Her recovery was difficult, yet the doctors were surprised at how quickly she recovered. At age seventeen, she was awarded the Nobel Peace Prize.
Bethany Hamilton	**C.** By the age of six, she was separated from her mother and sold into slavery. At thirteen, she suffered a head injury that almost killed her and resulted in her suffering from epilepsy. As an adult, she escaped slavery and led many others to freedom.
Harriet Tubman	**D.** His teachers said he was "too stupid to learn anything." As an inventor, he made one thousand unsuccessful attempts at inventing the light bulb. When a reporter asked, "How did it feel to fail 1,000 times?" he replied, "I didn't fail 1,000 times. The light bulb was an invention with 1,000 steps."
Thomas Edison	**E.** When he was in high school, he tried out for the basketball team and didn't make it. However, he became one of the most famous players in NBA history. He said, "I've missed more than nine thousand shots in my career. I've lost almost three hundred games. Twenty-six times, I've been trusted to take the game winning shot and missed. I've failed over and over and over again in my life. And that is why I succeed."

Are you still not sure who goes with which story? That's okay. Here are the answers: A is Bethany Hamilton. B is Malala Yousafzai. C is Harriet Tubman. D is Thomas Edison. E is Michael Jordan.

STRENGTHEN IT

Reread the stories. Underline the actions each person did that demonstrated resilience. Circle instances of bravery, persistence, and confidence.

Do you share any of the strengths displayed by these individuals? What are they? Write down one strength you share and one example of how you used it.

It's not just famous people, like the ones we mentioned, who are resilient. We all can be resilient. What's most important to know is that resilience helps us become powerful people who can support ourselves and others around us.

BONUS

(Do this activity with your special adult.)

Here's the first bonus activity for you to do! Work on it with your special adult—a parent, teacher, relative, or some other person who you know cares for you.

Interview someone you admire (they don't need to be famous) and ask them about a challenge they faced. Here are some questions you can ask them.

- What was something hard you overcame?
- What did you learn about yourself?
- What did you learn that could help others?
- What helped you succeed?

After finishing the interview, write down how that person demonstrated resilience. Write down some things that you learned.

Now you know resilience is important. It's especially important in helping you deal with stress you might be feeling. Let's learn more.

ACTIVITY 4

Stress: Helpful vs. Unhelpful

LEARN IT

We often think of stress as a bad thing. But did you know that not all stress is bad? Stress can be helpful and unhelpful.

Stress is helpful when it motivates you to do something better and achieve your goals. *Helpful stress* might be what you feel before you go to a birthday party where you won't know everyone, try a new sport, or give a class presentation. Anything that is new or difficult comes with some stress. Learning a new skill or lesson in school can be stressful, and also rewarding.

But sometimes, stress can be unhelpful. Stress can be unhelpful if you can't control what's causing it, if you have no breaks from it, or if you don't have any support to cope with it. Some people call this type of stress *toxic stress*. Toxic stress is when you experience things that are really hard and they overwhelm your ability to cope with them. (If this is something you're suffering from, talk to an adult who cares about you.)

There is also a third type of stress that is called *workable stress*. Workable stress falls between helpful and unhelpful stress. The situation you're in may still feel challenging. But you believe that you have more control over whatever's causing it or what you might do about it. And you're able to work with the stress to grow.

You might feel workable stress if you are going through something hard, but you have someone's support. For example, maybe you're learning remotely because of the COVID-19 pandemic or experiencing some other kind of crisis—and you have a grown-up nearby to help you.

What's neat about going through helpful and workable stress is that working through these stressors can help you grow as a person. You'll come out of the situation stronger, with new skills and abilities you can use during future challenges.

In order to cope better with stress, we'd like to give you some practice identifying types of stress.

DO IT

Here are some stories from kids who are going through different types of stress. Read each one and try to figure out whether the kid is going through *helpful stress*, *workable stress*, or *toxic stress*.

Erika tried out for a role in the school play. She started to cry and bombed the audition. When she found out she was in the ensemble (that she had a small part performing in a group), part of her wanted to quit, but she decided to stick with it.

Erika is going through ______________________________ stress.

Kiana has a science test on Monday, which is her hardest class. Over the weekend, she feels stressed when she thinks about the test, which motivates her to study a little bit each day. She saves extra time on Sunday to look over her materials. She aces her test.

Kiana is going through ______________________________ stress.

Jaden's classmates have been teasing him all year, every day. They call him a loser and make fun of his clothing. One kid calls him names and even pushes him, saying, "I'm just joking! Can't you take a joke, nerd?" Jaden is being bullied, and he's afraid to tell anyone or get help. He feels completely alone.

Jaden is going through ______________________ stress.

How did that go? Here are the answers.

Erika experienced **workable stress**. It wasn't fun to struggle in the audition, and it may not have been her first choice to have a small part, but she's committing to it, and she'll probably grow.

Kiana's case represents **helpful stress.** She felt some pressure because science is her hardest class, but that pressure made her more determined to study. And by studying, she achieved a good outcome.

Jaden is experiencing **toxic stress.** He's being bullied, and he's afraid to tell anyone about it. What he's going through is unfair and leaves him feeling alone and unprotected.

STRENGTHEN IT

You just learned a lot about stress. What stresses you out? Does it have to do with family, friends, school, or the world around you (your community)? Is it one big problem or a bunch of smaller problems that still feel like a lot to deal with? Below, draw or tell your stress story. If it helps, you may want to complete this activity with your special adult.

We know it can be hard to share your story. When bad things happen, you may feel sad, guilty, or embarrassed. However, it can make you feel better to tell your story. As you complete the activities in this book, keep this image or story in mind. Feel free to share your story with your special adult.

ACTIVITY 5

Toxic Stress

LEARN IT

In this activity, you will learn a little bit more about unhelpful, or toxic, stress, and its impact on your mind and body.

Again, toxic stress is when you have severe or prolonged problems—meaning there are a lot of them, and they don't stop—and they overwhelm your ability to cope.

It's not always easy to think or read about toxic stress. Sometimes kids feel embarrassed, guilty, or ashamed when bad things happen to them. Remember, all these feelings are normal—and even when painful things have occurred, both situations and people can change for the better. It's also really important for you to know that kids are never to blame if an adult does things to hurt them or if things in their families or the world around them feel too hard to bear. You are never the cause of any toxic stress you might feel.

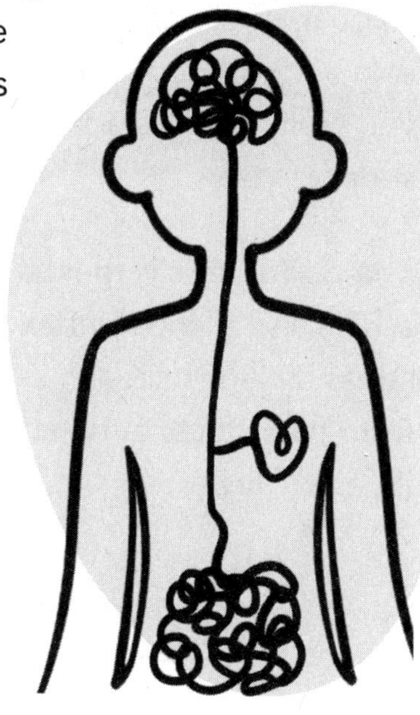

But it's important to learn about toxic stress and what you can do about it. Toxic stress is toxic because it's like poison, and it can lead to significant harm, both physically and emotionally.

If you have experienced very upsetting situations in your life, your body makes more stress hormones (natural chemicals in your brain) than it should. When you have too many stress hormones, you may be quick to be angry, act without thinking, or get overwhelmed easily. This is called being triggered.

When you're triggered, certain places, people, noises, and even smells can make you easily upset and overreact. And this can happen even after the stress itself ends. It is as if your mind and body keep a record of what happened, holding onto these negative events even after they are over. This makes it easy for you to overreact when something else happens that reminds you of those memories.

For example, Gabriel's parents have been fighting ever since his father lost his job. They yell so loudly it keeps Gabriel up at night. Sometimes, they even throw things. Now, Gabriel has noticed that if his teacher raises her voice a little, it makes him upset. Sometimes he goes under his desk or wants to throw something. He knows he shouldn't be acting this way, but he can't help himself.

This example describes how toxic stress can haunt you. It can make you feel angry, overwhelmed, and panicked. If you feel this way, know that there is nothing wrong with you. We promise you that, throughout this book, you will gain tools for dealing with these strong feelings.

If you're dealing with toxic stress, when you are ready, seek out an adult who feels safe and talk about what happened or is happening to you. We also recommend you complete this activity side by side with your special adult so your adult can support you.

The good news is that having safe, warm, and nurturing relationships with special adults and friends buffers you (a fancy word that means "protects") from toxic stress. Scientists teach us that there are certain experiences that can protect us from the effects of toxic stress. These are called positive childhood experiences (PCEs). They are:

- Feeling able to talk to your family about your feelings
- Feeling that your family is supportive during hard times
- Participating in community traditions
- Feeling like you belong in school
- Having support from friends
- Having at least two adults who aren't your parents who care about you
- Feeling safe and protected by an adult at home

DO IT

If you experience toxic stress, you can be easily triggered (just like Gabriel). If you haven't experienced toxic stress—if it doesn't feel like these questions apply to you—you can skip this activity. But if you have experienced toxic stress, these are important to answer. So, with your special adult, answer the following questions.

Are there certain situations, places, sights, sounds, smells, thoughts, or emotions that trigger you—that make you feel really angry, panicked, or overwhelmed? If yes, what are they?

STRENGTHEN IT

Now that you identified possible toxic stress triggers, can you create a plan for handling them? For each of your triggers, identify what the trigger is, what you usually do, and what you want to do instead.

For instance, Gabriel knows that when <u>his teacher raises her voice</u> (trigger), it makes him <u>want to jump under his desk or throw something</u> (what he usually does). But he also knows this is more because of his memories of his parents fighting than because the teacher's about to do something scary. So, he decides that if he's triggered by his teacher raising her voice in class, he'll <u>take a deep breath so he doesn't react right away</u> (what he wants to do instead).

Now, you try.

If I am triggered by: ____

I usually do: ____

Instead, I will do: ____

____

BONUS

(Do this activity with your special adult.)

Look over the list of positive childhood experiences (PCEs) in the "Learn It" section. Can you bring more of those into your life? For example, is there an event in your school or your community that you can participate in so you're not alone and so you have something nice to look forward to? What about talking with someone else about your feelings?

Write down some things from the list that will help you build a good support system when things get hard and reduce toxic stress.

I will try: ____

I will try: ____

I will try: ____

Keep your list handy so you can use your strategies right away. And remember, toxic stress is tough, so don't go through it alone. Talk to people who might be able to help you deal with what you're going through.

RESILIENCE CHECKPOINT

Congratulations! You have come to the first checkpoint. You have already learned so much! Here's a quick summary of what we hope you learned:

- What resilience is
- Why resilience is important
- How resilient you are right now
- What helpful stress, workable stress, and toxic stress are
- How toxic stress can affect you and how to deal with it

We introduced you to a lot of vocabulary words in part 1, like "resilience" and "stress." Here's a fun way to help that vocabulary stick. In the puzzle, find the words you came across in part 1, which are listed below. The words can appear going across, up or down, and even backward. You may need a little resilience to find them, and we know you can do it. (But if you need to see the answers, you'll find them in the answer key at the back of the book.)

OUR UNSINKABLE BOAT

A
N D
S C V
L O P E
A N U L R
O T F J E S
G R O W T H I
S O M H G U O T
S L I S T E N H Y
E Y E N R U O J H
R
E C N E D I F N O C T R E S I L I E N C E
C K V F R I E N D S D G N I P O C E V
N F L E X I B I L I T Y P M P V A
U T D E T A R E P O O C L G R
O K E E P G O I N G G A B
B O P T I M I S T I C

ADVERSITY	CONTROL	GOALS	LISTEN
BOUNCE	COOPERATE	GROWTH	OPTIMISTIC
BRAVE	COPING	HELP	RESILIENCE
CALM	FLEXIBILITY	JOURNEY	STRESS
CONFIDENCE	FRIENDS	KEEP GOING	TOUGH

Way to go! You've made it through the checkpoint! Now let's move forward and learn about making emotions your friends.

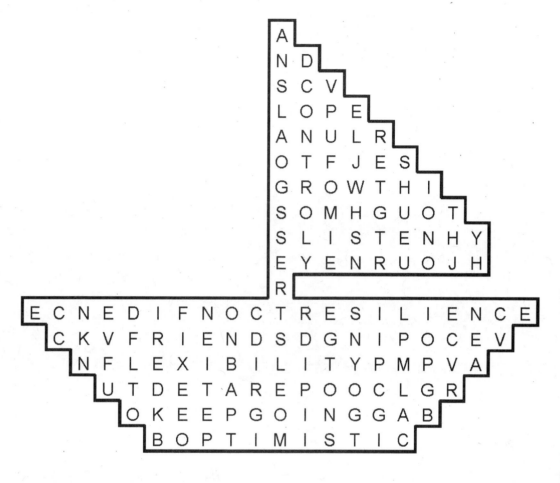

PART 2

Making Emotions Your Friends

"Feelings are much like waves. We can't stop them from coming, but we can choose which one to surf."

—Jonathan Mårtensson

WHAT YOU'LL DISCOVER

Welcome to part 2 of the book, which is about making emotions your friends. How are you feeling right now? Relaxed, confident, interested? Tired, bored, annoyed? While we hope you're not feeling uncomfortable emotions right now, like sadness, frustration, or rage, all emotions have value and can teach you something. And understanding the emotions you feel helps you be resilient.

In part 2, you will learn:

- How to name your emotions
- Where emotions live in your body
- How to understand and accept all emotions, even the yucky ones
- How to pump up your positive emotions to increase flexibility, problem solving, and well-being
- How to develop an attitude of gratitude
- How to pay attention to what's happening to you right now with acceptance and without judgment
- How to be kind to yourself

ACTIVITY 6

Naming Emotions to Tame Them

LEARN IT

Feelings can be sorted into two categories. One is positive or comfortable feelings—feelings you like and want more of. The other is negative or uncomfortable feelings—the feelings you often don't like and want to get rid of. Negative feelings are often unpleasant. But in the end, all feelings are normal, and they all give you important information.

You can also be more specific with your feelings than just calling them positive or negative. Each positive or negative feeling you have has its own name or label. When you can describe your emotions with precise words, you will know what you want to do with them. Isn't that cool?

For example, if you are feeling upset, you may be feeling sad, mad, or guilty. Even though all these different types of upset may feel negative or uncomfortable, each emotion is slightly different from the others. And what you want to do about each one is probably different too. If you're sad, for example, you might want to talk to a friend. But if you're mad, you might want to hit a pillow to let your energy out. In other words, what helps when you are sad may be different from what helps when you are mad.

In the end, the more specific you can be with how you name your emotions, the better able you'll be to cope or tame them. This is an essential step in building resilience.

DO IT

Below are feeling faces. First, identify which of the feelings are comfortable and which are uncomfortable by circling the positive feeling faces and underlining the negative feeling faces. Then, write down the feeling word that goes with each face from the list on the next page.

1. ________________

2. ________________

3. ________________

4. ________________

5. ________________

6. ________________

7. ________________

8. ________________

9. ________________

FEELING WORDS:

silly	angry	worried
sad	embarrassed	surprised
excited	lonely	happy

The answers, if you need to see them, are at the bottom of this page.

Are there other feelings you can think of that aren't listed? Try to think of two feelings and draw the faces that might go with each.

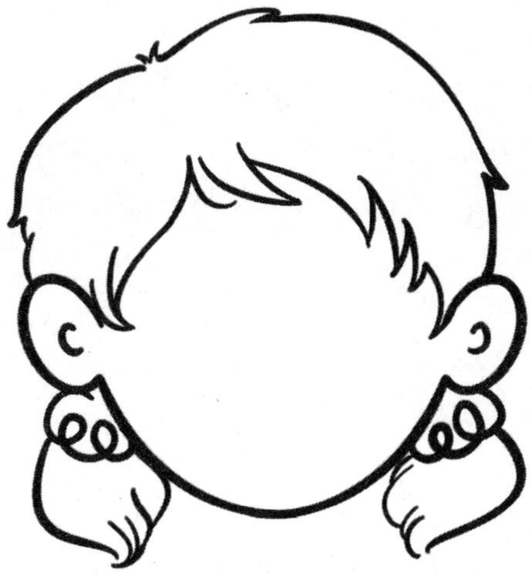

Feeling: ______________________

Feeling: ______________________

1. Angry. 2. Lonely. 3. Happy. 4. Excited. 5. Worried. 6. Surprised. 7. Embarrassed. 8. Sad. 9. Silly.

BONUS

(Do this activity with your special adult.)

You have many feelings each and every day. Use this game of tic-tac-toe to help name your feelings and talk about how each one feels.

Figure out which of you is going to be player X and which of you is going to be player O. When it's your turn, put your symbol (X or O) on a square, and share a time when you felt that feeling. For example, if you put your symbol on the "scared" face, you can say, "I felt scared when my grandmother was sick." Let your partner know whether the feeling was a positive feeling or a negative feeling.

The first player to draw their symbol on three squares in a row, whether it's horizontal (straight across), vertical (up and down), or diagonal (running from one corner to the other), wins the game.

This will help you practice how to name your feelings—the first step to taming them.

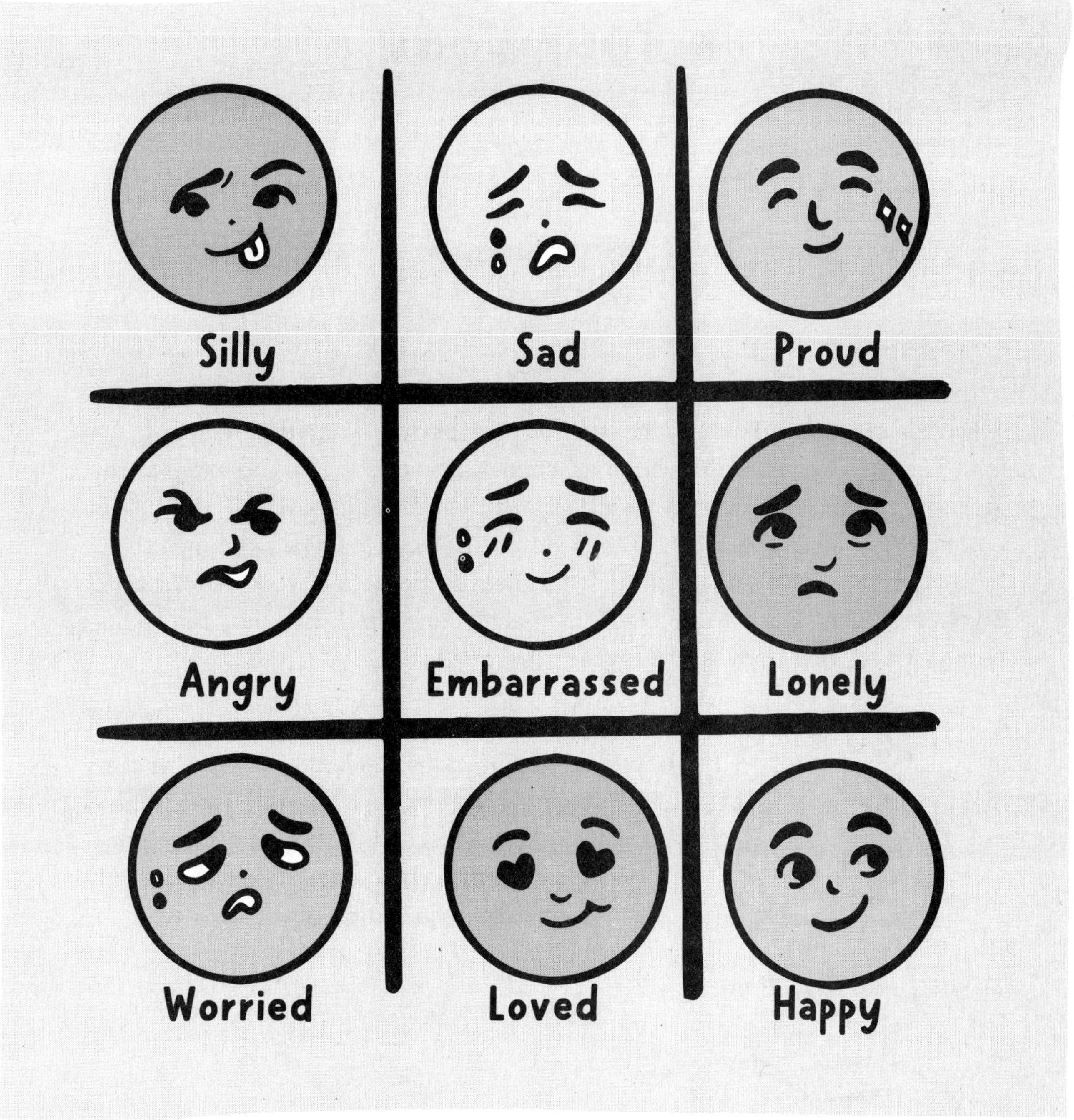
Silly
Sad
Proud
Angry
Embarrassed
Lonely
Worried
Loved
Happy

ACTIVITY 7

Feeling Emotions in Your Body

LEARN IT

In the last activity, you practiced naming your feelings (the *what* of feelings), which is a step toward taming those feelings, especially when they're strong. In this activity, we would like you to practice discovering *where* you experience feelings in your body and *how* your body feels while you're having a particular emotion. Some kids feel worry in their stomachs. It can feel like a tummy ache, butterflies, or a knot. Anger can be felt as heat at the back of your neck or ears. Sometimes when kids have big feelings that feel uncontrollable, they can feel numb all over their body, as if they can't feel anything.

By knowing *where* and *how* you feel emotions in your body, you can use these feeling sensations as clues that you are experiencing a strong feeling. With this awareness, you can then create a coping plan. This helps you take charge of your emotions, rather than letting them take charge of you!

DO IT

Read the story below. While reading it, underline all Zoe's emotions. Then, go back and reread. Circle where and how she feels them in her body. We did the first ones for you.

Zoe is ready to have lunch at school. The cafeteria is always loud, which makes her feel a little anxious, and her heart beats faster. Zoe always sits with Marika, Gemma, and Sydney, but today she finds Sarah sitting in her seat. Sydney says, "Sorry, Zoe. I need to eat with Sarah today, so she has to sit here." Zoe feels her face get hot with embarrassment. The girls keep talking with each other while Zoe stands there, not sure what to do. Zoe feels mad and squeezes her eyebrows together, feeling anger rise from her eyes to the top of her head. She doesn't know where to sit, and she begins to feel an achy, uncomfortable feeling in her belly.

STRENGTHEN IT

Here is a list of common emotions. Close your eyes and imagine having that emotion. Where do you feel that emotion in your body? Color in that place on the body diagram. Use a different color for each emotion so you create a rainbow of emotions.

happiness	excitement	worry
anger	sadness	embarrassment

BONUS

(Do this activity with your special adult.)

Ask a trusted adult where they feel these emotions. Color in the places they tell you about in the body diagram below. Do they feel the emotions in the same places you do?

Even though your special adult may feel stress in different parts of their body, we *all can use these physical sensations we experience in our bodies to help us.* Instead of fighting our emotions, we can let them guide us (like a GPS on our boat) to safe shores.

ACTIVITY 8

Accepting the "Yuck"

LEARN IT

Congratulations! You've learned to name your feelings and find where you feel them in your body. This means you are beginning to use your emotions to direct you, like a captain uses a map to get to a faraway land.

It's important to learn that all feelings, even the yucky ones, are beneficial. *What?* you ask. *Yucky feelings are helpful?* Yes!

Of course, feelings like happiness, excitement, and calm are comfortable, and you like them. But feelings like sadness, anger, and worry are helpful too. Sometimes they tell you something's wrong that you need to fix. For example, if you feel angry when someone cuts in front of you in the lunch line, it's a sign that you feel something unfair has happened. Yucky feelings can also be a sign that you care. For example, if you get nervous when a teacher calls on you in class, that can be a sign you want to get things right.

Some of the yucky things we feel, like stress that just won't stop, are really unpleasant. But experiencing yucky emotions in smaller doses can make you stronger when really yucky things come up. So, instead of trying to ignore, push away, or get stuck in yucky feelings, let's embrace the yuck and build skills for dealing with all the emotions we feel!

Check out the acronym below to help you "accept the yuck."

Y. You take a deep breath, notice the feeling you don't like is real, and realize it's not going to change immediately.

U. Understand that uncomfortable feelings aren't dangerous, they can be helpful, and often, they will soon pass.

C. Choose to say, "This will pass," instead of, "I can't stand it," or "It's not fair."

K. Know that you can share how you're feeling with someone who cares.

Keep in mind that accepting what you feel isn't the same as liking what you're feeling. Acceptance also doesn't mean denying your feelings by pretending they aren't there. Acceptance means not fighting the way you feel. In the end, fighting your yucky emotions will only get you more stuck in the yuck.

DO IT

Think about a time in the past when you had a yucky feeling. Were you able to accept it? If so, how? If you weren't able to accept the yucky feeling then, try thinking about how you *would* accept it, knowing what you know about feelings now.

It can help to try to "notice" your feelings, instead of treating yourself *as* your feelings, which is what we do when we say things like, "I *am* stressed." Stay away from "I am" and instead state, "I notice I am feeling…"

Example: "I notice I am feeling worried about going back to school. I will remind myself that these feelings will pass and talk with my teacher."

When you create a separation between your thoughts and yourself in this way, the feeling of stress seems more temporary. It seems like something you can look at from the outside, and even change.

Your turn.

STRENGTHEN IT

Think about a time you felt each of the yucky feelings listed below. Write down something you learned from feeling the yuck. Knowing what you can learn from the yuck can make it easier to accept the yuck in the future and respond to it in ways that are resilient and strong. See the example we provided for sadness to help you with this exercise.

The Yucky Feeling	What It Might Teach or Tell You	When You Felt This Yucky Feeling	What You Learned from Feeling the Yuck
Sadness	Sadness can remind you of who and what matters to you.	My dog died last year.	I learned that I was sad because I loved my dog.
Anger	Anger can make you feel motivated to fix something that is not right.		
Guilt	Guilt can teach you to not make the same mistake twice.		

Worry	Worry can keep you safe by not letting you make risky choices. It can make you focus more carefully and have a plan.		

BONUS

(Do this one with your special adult.)

Coping with big emotions is kind of like surfing a wave. The wave starts, and it grows really big—and in time, it passes. The water levels back out again. You just have to keep your surfboard steady.

Ask your special adult what big waves they've faced. How were they able to accept the yuck and keep their surfboard steady? What advice can they share with you?

Then, on the next page, draw a picture of yourself surfing a big wave. Share a piece of advice with the surfer (that's you). Put the advice underneath the picture. For example: "Uncomfortable feelings are normal, and I will feel better soon." Visualize yourself on the surfboard as you ride the waves, taking your piece of advice. And notice that just like the waves, big emotions pass.

My advice to myself: ______________________________

ACTIVITY 9

Pumping Up Positive Emotions

LEARN IT

We all tend to hold on to negative emotions, like sadness or anger, and forget the positive ones we feel, like joy or hope. But noticing and creating positive emotions has many benefits.

Positive emotions help you be flexible in how you think. They also help you solve problems better, connect with people you love, and deal with things that are stressful—and even grow from that stress. Positive emotions can even help you feel better in your body because they improve your immune system—your body's way of fighting germs—and help you recover when you're hurt.

Again, all your emotions are important. They all tell you things. And it isn't possible to get rid of all your negative emotions. You probably wouldn't want to either because your negative emotions sometimes let you know about things you need to watch out for.

In the end, the key to being healthy and resilient is to *balance* the emotions you feel. Scientists have discovered that if you feel *three* positive feelings for every time you feel *one* negative feeling, you'll end up at your strongest.

So, how can you use positive emotions to be more resilient—especially when you're dealing with a lot of stress? You can PUMP!

P. Pump up positive experiences for yourself. Do something fun. Have a laugh. Do something nice for someone else.

U. Understand the *negative bias* we all have. We tend to remember negative things more than positive ones. Instead, pay attention to the good things in your world and inside of you. So often, you might hardly notice positive emotions and events, while negative feelings stick with you like gum on the bottom of your shoe. Instead of dwelling on negative emotions, savor positive emotions and experiences, like a good grade you get in school or a fun day you spend with a friend or a family member.

M. Make it a movie. Watch and replay the positive memories you have created in your mind. Savor them—remember, as clearly as you can, all the little details and the good feelings. You might be surprised at how much you can feel those same positive emotions again just by thinking about them!

P. Pay attention to the goodness in your world. Notice the caring of others. And notice your own good qualities—the parts of you that you're proud of. By doing so, you'll create powerful positive emotions.

DO IT

It's often hard to remember the positive emotions we feel unless we make an effort to notice and remember them. Look at the list of positive emotions in the chart. Each day over the next week, put a check next to any positive emotion you felt that day. See if you can experience at least three positive emotions each day to balance out any negative emotions you might have felt.

	Mon	Tue	Wed	Thu	Fri	Sat	Sun
Happy							
Silly							
Grateful							
Optimistic							
Loving							
Hopeful							
Proud							
Interested							
Calm							
Excited							
Other:							

STRENGTHEN IT

Not all our happy moments have to be big ones. Even super-simple things can boost your mood and make you feel better, like getting a smile or meeting someone's eyes and saying "thank you." These are what scientists call "micro-moments" of connection. These short, simple moments of connection to others improve your happiness, your health, and your ability to be resilient.

For the next week, try to notice or create micro-moments with three different people each day. Write down in the boxes below the micro-moment you experienced and how it made you feel. Use the example as a guide.

	Person 1: Mom	Person 2: My sister	Person 3: My teacher
Monday 	She left me a nice note with my lunch.	I told her, "Thank you," when she let me use her tablet.	I said, "Good morning," to my teacher in the morning.

	Person 1:	Person 2:	Person 3:
Monday			
Tuesday			
Wednesday			
Thursday			
Friday			
Saturday			
Sunday			

BONUS

(Do this one with your special adult.)

Laughing and having fun are positive emotions that improve your health, mood, and coping. Try out laughing yoga with your special adult.

To begin, stand up and start wiggling while you look into your special adult's eyes (that might already start you laughing).

Then you and your special adult should say, "HA, HA, HE, HE, HO, HO." See if the laughter can come all the way from your belly.

Next, try a silent laugh. Laugh, but don't make any sounds.

Enjoy the laughter and notice how this activity makes you and your special adult smile from ear to ear.

ACTIVITY 10

Developing an Attitude of Gratitude

LEARN IT

Another powerful way to increase positive emotions and to feel more resilient is by building an attitude of gratitude. Being grateful means *noticing the good* in your life and in the world around you and *being thankful* for it. Grateful people feel more positive emotions, such as love, joy, and hope, and fewer negative emotions, such as anger, frustration, and bitterness. People who practice gratitude tend to be happier, less sad, and more resilient.

Gratitude can also help you get through difficult times. When you face an obstacle, part of your brain, the amygdala, can shut down the logical part of your brain—the part where you think, organize information, and solve problems. Practicing gratitude calms the amygdala. It can help you think more clearly so you can find ways to solve challenges, stay calm, and move forward.

DO IT

1. Tonight, before you go to bed, look back at your day.
2. Focus on *three* things that went well for you—three positive things that happened. They can be big, or they can be small, such as getting a good seat on the bus, laughing with a friend at lunch, or eating a yummy dinner.
3. Write down the three positive events. Try to be specific. For example, it's better to write down, "I am grateful for getting a good seat on the bus," than to write, "I am grateful for the bus."

____

____

____

____

____

4. Then reflect on and savor the memory of all three of these events. See them like a movie in your head. Watch them again (like a rerun), remembering how good they were.
5. The next day, review what you wrote. Notice how good you feel.

If you find this helpful, make gratitude a habit! You can get yourself a notebook or a gratitude journal and jot down positive events to savor every day. Over time, you'll notice your gratitude and resilience muscles getting stronger.

STRENGTHEN IT

Write a letter to someone in your life you feel grateful for. It could be a friend, family member, teacher, or other special adult. Thank that person for what they have done. Be specific and tell them why you are grateful and how they made a difference in your life.

You can also read your letter out loud to them. Not only will you make the person's day, but you'll make your own day too.

ACTIVITY 11

Staying Present and Mindful

LEARN IT

Did you know that people who are able to hold on to positive emotions often practice mindfulness? But what is mindfulness?

Mindfulness is accepting your thoughts and feelings for what they are, without trying to change them or expecting them to be different. It is also about becoming aware of your five senses (what you see, hear, touch, smell, and taste) and of how your body feels and moves. It means noticing what is happening right now and truly being present without judgment.

This may sound hard. But like resilience, it's a skill you can develop with practice.

Often, your body is in the present, but your mind is not. Your mind is terrific at time traveling! Time traveling is when you are thinking about the past or the future and not the present. For example, you might be thinking about your parents fighting at breakfast or the big test coming up next week. But you can teach your mind to stay in the right-now. And when you do, it's easier to get unstuck from the yuck of uncomfortable feelings.

DO IT

Learning to ride the waves of life is something we have talked about a lot. Let's now combine that with breathing deeply and slowly. Breathing deeply and slowly often makes it easier to ride the waves of life—those moments when things are tough or when what you feel is overwhelming—especially when they get really intense.

So, pretend you're a surfer riding the waves of life. Breathe in as you go up the wave, counting slowly: 1, 2, 3. Pretend to balance your body on the wave and pause at the top of the wave, counting: 4, 5. Then, breathe out as you go down the wave, counting: 6, 7, 8, 9, 10. Breathing this way helps you to surf the waves of life.

STRENGTHEN IT

Try a mindfulness activity with your pet or stuffed animal. Pets are great because they naturally calm us down and give us support. And stuffed animals do this too, especially for those of us who don't have pets. You will use four out of your five senses with your pet or animal: seeing, hearing, touching, and smelling. (We're not going to ask you to taste your pet or stuffed animal!)

1. Sit down with your pet or stuffed animal and take three long and deep breaths.
2. Now really look at your pet or stuffed animal.
3. Notice what you *see*. How big is your pet or stuffed animal? What color is it? What does its fur look like? Its nose or tongue?
4. What do you *hear*? Does your pet make any noise? If you are using a stuffed animal, does it squeak or make a noise when you touch it?
5. Does your pet have a unique *smell*? Does your stuffed animal smell yummy or yucky?
6. Now *feel* your pet or stuffed animal. What do you feel? Is your pet or stuffed animal soft, furry, or smooth?

BONUS

(Do this one with your special adult.)

Help the captain of the ship reach the treasure by gathering the letters you find along the way. Place them on the spaces below the maze to receive important advice for navigating life's ups and downs.

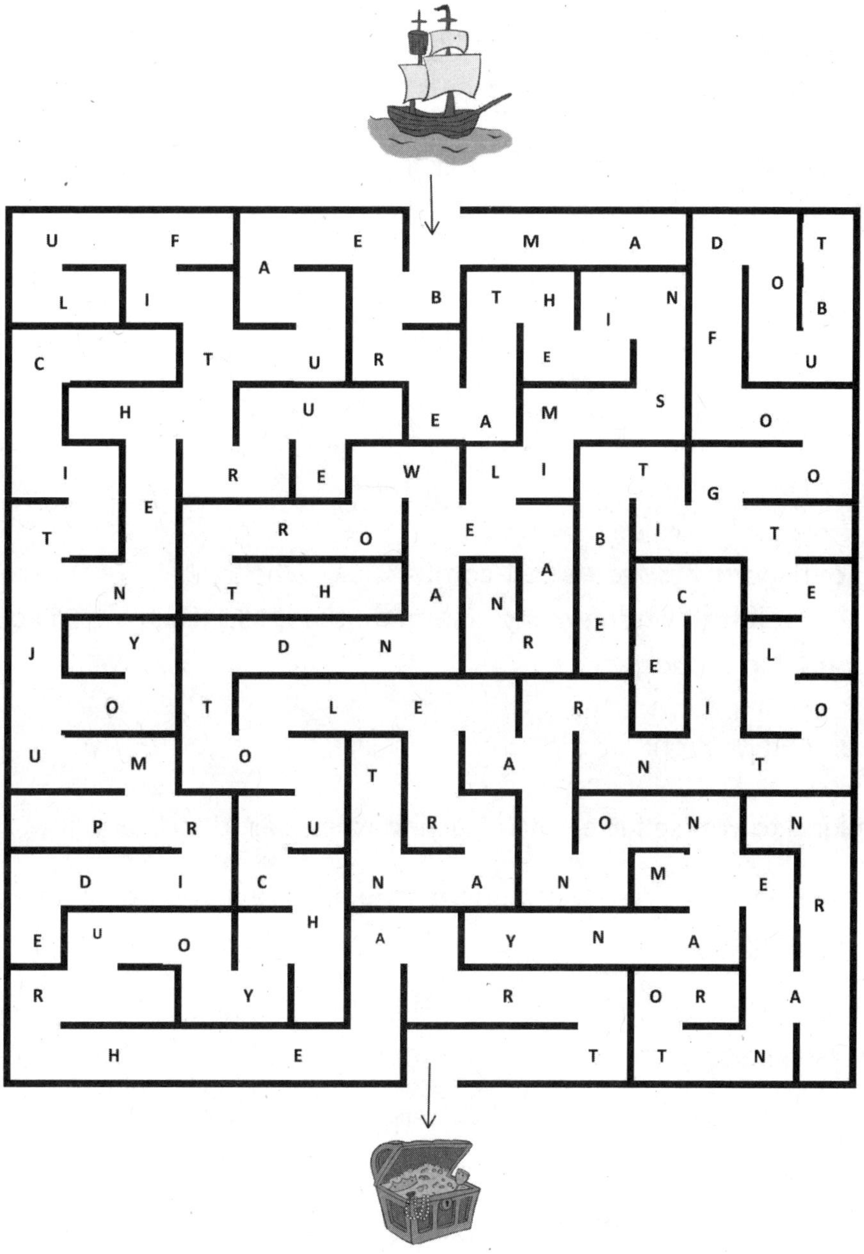

___ ___ ___ ___ ___ ___ ___ ___   ___ ___,   ___ ___ ___ ___ ___,   ___ ___ ___

___ ___ ___ ___ ___ ___   ___ ___ ___ ___ ___   ___ ___ ___ ___ ___.

Did you get the answer? (If you struggled with it, you'll find the answer at the very bottom of this page.) Think of someone you would like to share this advice with.

Answer: Breathe in, smile, and touch your heart.

ACTIVITY 12

Being Your Own Best Friend

LEARN IT

One type of mindful practice is self-compassion. When you have self-compassion, you treat yourself with kindness and understanding, especially when you're going through something tough.

To have self-compassion:

- Be kind to yourself like you'd be kind to a dear friend.
- Notice when you're having a hard time and treat yourself with warmth and understanding.
- When you make a mistake, and we all make mistakes, try not to judge yourself harshly.
- When you feel hurt, tell yourself, "This is really difficult right now." Ask yourself, "How can I care for myself in this moment?"
- Realize that suffering, making mistakes, and not being perfect are what make us human.

Things will not always go the way you want them to. You will experience frustration and losses, make mistakes, and fall short of your goals. Despite all these challenges, we encourage you to open your heart and be a great best friend for yourself! Often, you'll find that this makes it easier to get through the hard times.

DO IT

The loving-kindness meditation is a practice of directing kindness and positive thoughts to yourself.

Start off by saying,

May I be happy.

May I be safe.

May I be strong.

May I live with ease and in peace.

Now try this:

When you breathe in, *smile.*

When you breathe out, say, "*May I be happy.*"

When you breathe in, *think of something that comforts you.*

When you breathe out, say, "*May I be safe.*"

When you breathe in, *imagine yourself having courage.*

When you breathe out, say, "*May I be strong.*"

When you breathe in, *imagine you're lying on a raft in calm waters.*

When you breathe out, say, "*May I live with ease and in peace.*"

How was that? You may want to print or write out the lines of the meditation and put them in a place you can see them, to remind you to be loving and kind to yourself.

STRENGTHEN IT

During the next week, keep an eye out for times when things get hard. Maybe someone does something to you that you don't like. Or maybe you make a mistake and you become super hard on yourself. In those moments, see if you can remember your self-compassion skills: the love you have for yourself and your desire to be at ease and in peace.

Then, jot down some thoughts below about the experience. Were you able to use your skills? If yes, did it help you to feel better by being kind to yourself? If not, why was it hard to be compassionate?

BONUS

(Do this one with your special adult.)

You just practiced self-compassion. It's also helpful to show compassion to others. Say to your special adult, "May you be healthy. May you be peaceful. May you be happy."

Then send loving-kindness to someone in your family. Say the name of the person first and then say, "__________________________________ (name of person), May you be healthy. May you be peaceful. May you be happy."

Lastly, choose anyone in the world and repeat the phrases for them.

Both self-compassion and compassion for others help you be kind to yourself and other people, feel more confident, cope with setbacks, and be willing to try hard things—all essential tools for growing your resilience.

RESILIENCE CHECKPOINT

Way to go! You've reached your second checkpoint. We hope you're feeling good. Here's a quick summary of what we hope you've learned:

- How to name your emotions or feelings
- Where you feel your emotions in your body
- How you can accept all the emotions that you feel, even the yucky ones
- How to pump up your positive emotions, including laughter and having fun
- How to develop an attitude of gratitude
- What mindfulness is and how to increase it
- How to develop kindness for yourself and others
- Ways to make emotions your friends

A Little Review with a Quick True-False Quiz

1. Naming your emotions helps you manage or "tame" them.	TRUE	FALSE
2. Emotions often cause a physical sensation in the body.	TRUE	FALSE
3. You should experience one positive feeling to balance one negative feeling.	TRUE	FALSE
4. Being mindful means staying in the moment without judgment.	TRUE	FALSE
5. You should always try to avoid feeling angry or sad.	TRUE	FALSE
6. Self-compassion means being mean to yourself.	TRUE	FALSE

Answers:

1. **True!** By naming your emotions, you can be specific about how you are feeling, which lets you think more clearly about why you are having those feelings and decide what you want to do with them.

2. **True!** Emotions are signals in your brain that cause sensations in your body. Sensations in your body can also cause emotions.

3. **False!** Try to have *three positive feelings* for every negative feeling. This helps build your resilience.

4. **True!** By teaching your mind to stay here, without judgment, it's easier to get unstuck from the yuck of uncomfortable feelings

5. **False!** Feeling uncomfortable emotions, like anger or sadness, is natural. By embracing the yuck, you can get helpful information.

6. **False!** Self-compassion means treating yourself kindly as you would a friend.

What's Left? Puzzle

Eliminate words from the grid until the remaining words—when read from left to right, row by row—spell out an important message. This puzzle can be a little tricky and requires patience, a skill that is so important in building resilience!

1. Cross off all words that end in a Y in columns A and C.
2. Cross off all words that contain a double letter in columns B and C.
3. Cross off all words that contain the word "US."
4. Cross off all one-syllable words in odd-numbered rows.
5. Cross off all words that contain an X.
6. Cross off all colors.

	A	B	C	D
1	ACCEPT	HAPPY	SAD	TIMES
2	EXCITED	BLUE	GUILTY	ALL
3	EMOTIONS	BORED	CONFUSED	MAROON
4	YELLOW	SILLY	EVEN	JEALOUS
5	LONELY	DISGUSTED	PROUD	EXPERIENCE
6	NERVOUS	THE	EMBARRASSED	EXCELLENT
7	ANGRY	SCARED	ANNOYED	MUSIC
8	FRUSTRATED	NEXT	GRUMPY	YUCKY
9	PURPLE	CHEERFUL	FEELINGS	AWED
10	ONES	MIXED	WORRIED	GREEN

The secret message is ____

Did you discover the secret message? (You'll find it at the bottom of this page.) That's right—it's important to accept all your emotions, even the yucky ones.

In the next part, you'll learn all about how you can use your feelings to unlock your thinking, achieve your goals, and be more resilient.

Okay, let's start thinking!

Answer: Accept all emotions, even the yucky ones.

PART 3

Creating Resilient Thinking

"Change your thoughts and you change your world."

—Norman Vincent Peale

WHAT YOU'LL DISCOVER

Part 3 of the book is about understanding how the ways you think affect the ways you feel—another important step in building resilience.

In this section, you will:

- Learn the relationship between your thoughts, feelings, and actions
- Discover your "thinking traps"
- Challenge unhelpful thinking
- Build optimism and a growth mindset
- Tap into what is important to you
- Learn to "fail forward"

Are you ready to develop resilient thinking? Let's go!

ACTIVITY 13

Thinking, Feeling, and Doing

LEARN IT

Picture a triangular sail, the kind you find on a sailboat. Imagine your feelings in one corner of the sail, your thoughts in another, and your actions in the other.

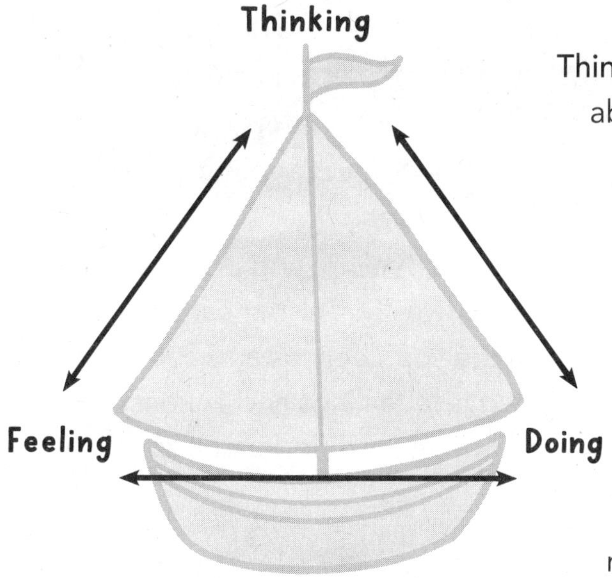

Thinking. Your thoughts are what you think about and what you say to yourself. For example, if you find out that your dad lost his job, you might think, *Oh no, we're going to be poor, maybe even homeless!*

Feeling. Your feelings are your emotions or how you feel, and they're affected by your thoughts. In the situation described above, you might feel scared and embarrassed about your dad's job loss.

Doing. Doing refers to the actions you take based on your feelings. In this situation, you might stop hanging out with your friends, especially when they do an activity that costs money, like going to the movies.

Here's how the example above would look.

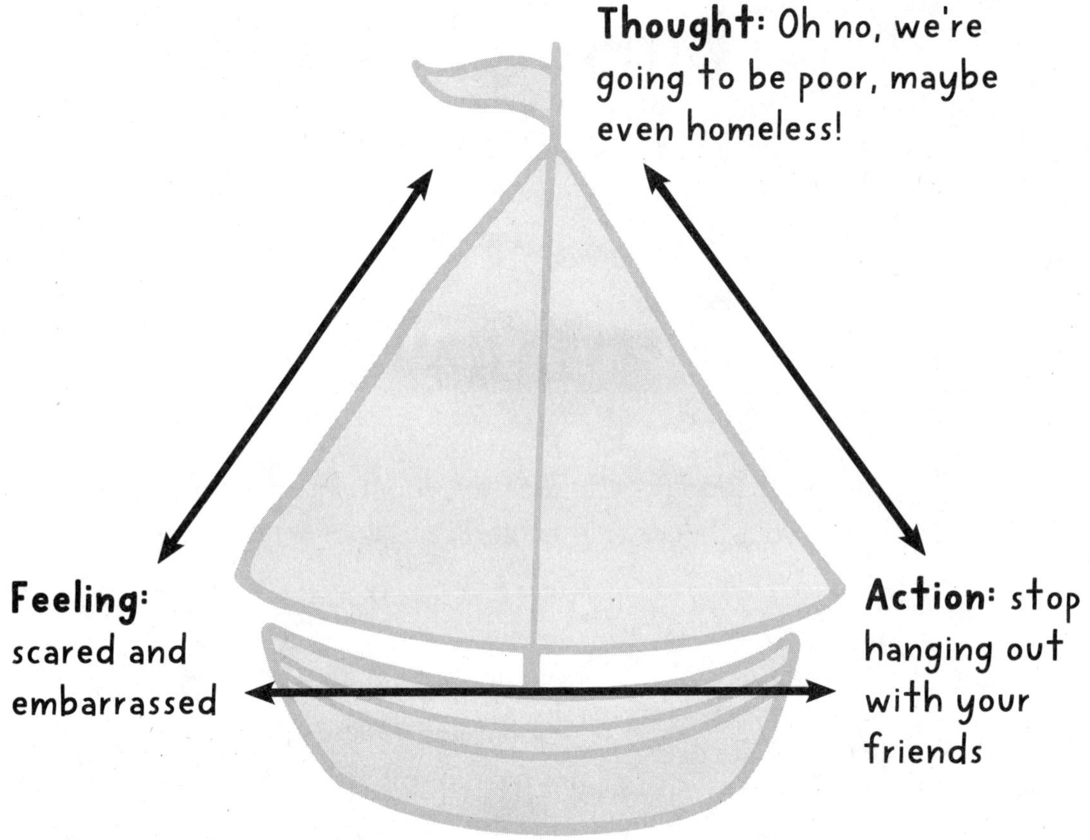
Thought: Oh no, we're going to be poor, maybe even homeless!
Feeling: scared and embarrassed
Action: stop hanging out with your friends

Do you see how the corners of the triangle—thinking, feeling, and doing—are all related? If one changes, it can change the other two. This also means that changing your thinking is a powerful way to change your feelings and actions. Just as thinking in a negative way can lead to negative feelings and actions, thinking in a more positive way can help you feel better and figure out good ways to handle things you're going through.

Let's look at another example. See if you can notice the relationship between thinking, feeling, and doing. It's the Fourth of July, and you and your family are invited to go out on the ocean in a sailboat. You are all having a good time, but then the sky starts to turn dark and gloomy. You get a pit in your stomach and feel nervous. That feeling then makes you think, *The sky looks dark. We better go back.* You and your family then act quickly and decide to head back before it starts to pour. And true enough, it starts to rain hard!

Do you see how your feelings affected your thinking and actions? In this example, you felt nervous, but instead of thinking negatively, your thinking was positive and helpful. Your thinking led to resilient behavior (problem solving and being effective) and a positive action (going back). What if your thinking was, *Oh no, it's going to rain, and we're going to drown!* Do you see how your thinking would lead to a negative feeling, like panicking, that could then lead to a negative consequence like a boat full of water?

Let's turn this boat around by getting good at identifying thoughts, feelings, and actions.

DO IT

Is it a thought, feeling, or action? Sometimes it's hard to tell the difference between your thinking, feeling, and doing. Let's practice breaking these down.

Put a circle around the thoughts.

Put a line under the feelings.

Put an X through the actions.

Sad	Talking to a friend	Everyone hates me.
Happy	I'm getting better.	It's terrible.
Worried	Taking a walk	Yelling at your mom
Taking a deep breath	Angry	What's wrong with me?
Scared	Calm	I can do it!

STRENGTHEN IT

Let's apply what you learned about thinking, feeling, and doing to your own life. Think about a situation that was challenging for you. What did you think, feel, and do during that time?

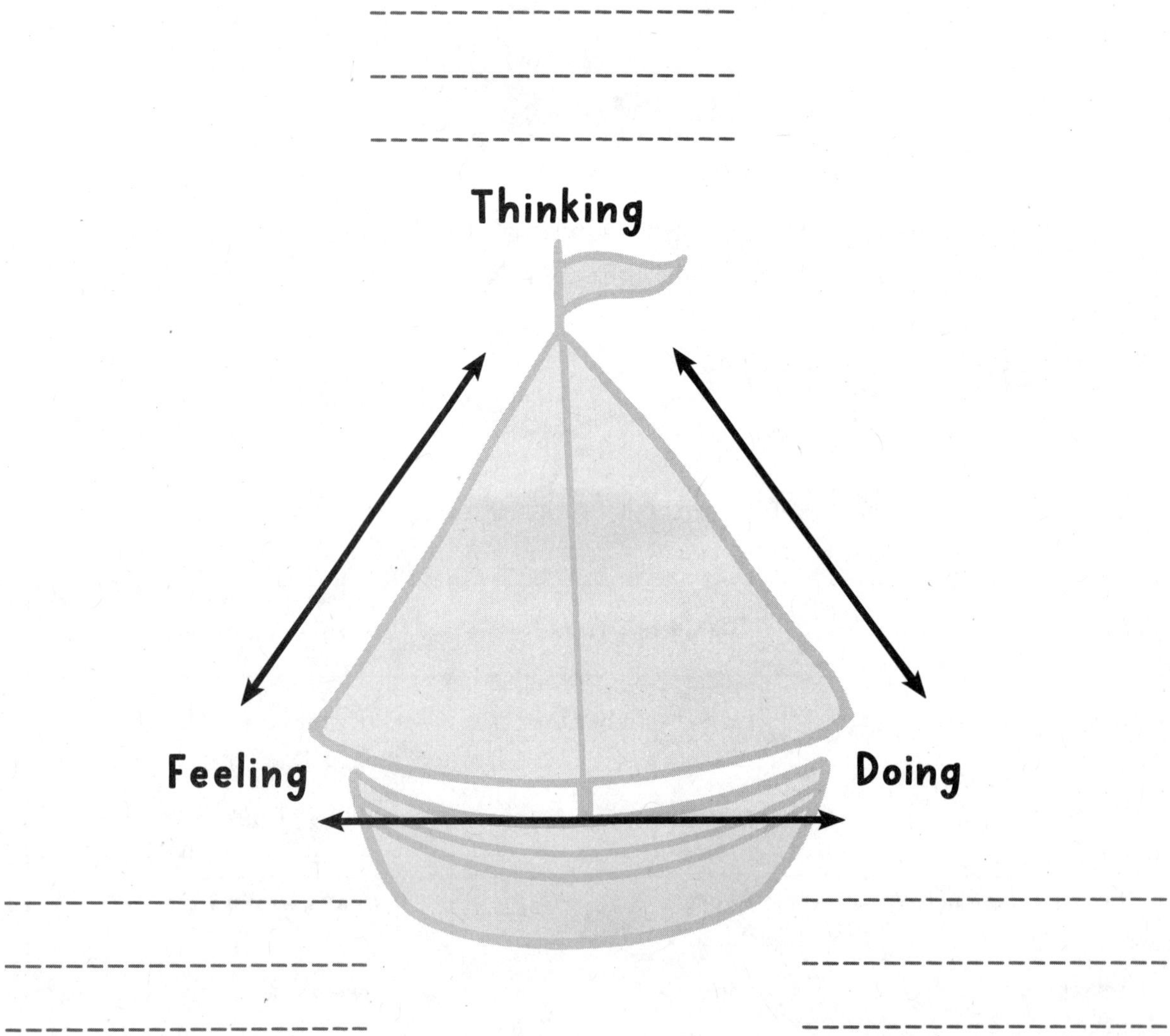

BONUS

(Do this one with your special adult.)

Ask your trusted adult to share with you a time when they faced a challenging situation. Ask them to write down what they thought, felt, and did when they were in that situation. See? Even your special adult has gone through difficult times! It can help to remember that you are not alone in facing challenges.

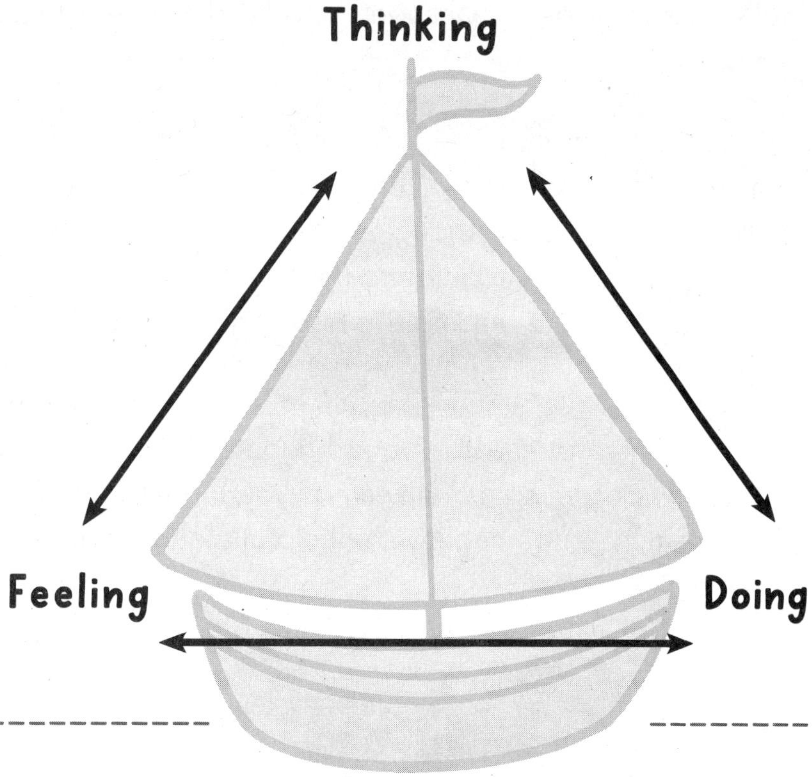

ACTIVITY 14

Discovering Your Thinking Traps

LEARN IT

Often people think the situations they're in make them feel a certain way. For example, say that having to move to a new school (the situation) is making you sad (the feeling). However, it is the way you *think* about the situation (*Moving is going to be awful* versus *It will be a challenge—and I can handle it*) that has the greatest influence on how you feel.

Many times, what you think or say to yourself is not true. It can be tricky because your thoughts can seem true, especially when you're feeling a strong negative emotion. But just because you have a thought, that doesn't make it true. For instance, we could think, *We're never going to finish writing this book*, but, you see, that's not true because you're reading this book right now! So, a thought is not a fact!

In this activity, you will bring awareness to your thoughts, the same way you did with your feelings. By becoming more aware of your negative thoughts, or "thinking traps," you can challenge negative, unhelpful thoughts and replace them with positive, helpful ones.

DO IT

Here are some of the common thinking traps we tend to fall into.

The Magnifier		All problems seem bigger or magnified.
Black-and-White Thinking		Seeing things as only right or wrong, good, or bad, perfect or terrible.
Mind-Reading		Guessing what others are thinking and assuming it's bad.
Emotional Reasoning		Believing that if you feel something strongly, it must be so.
Fortune Telling		Predicting the future and usually in a negative way.
Discounting the Positives		Believing the positive things that happen to you don't count.
"Should Statements"		Telling yourself how you "should" or "must" act.

Let's practice identifying these traps. First, use the key below to assign a different color to each type of thinking trap.

Red	Orange	Yellow	Green	Blue	Purple	Pink
The Magnifier	Black-and-White Thinking	Mind Reading	Emotional Reasoning	Fortune Telling	Discounting the Positives	Should Statements

Then, color the thinking traps you see in the thought bubbles.

I shouldn't have to socially distance myself from my friends. It shouldn't be taking so long to get back to normal from the pandemic.

Color: Pink

I made the basketball team and got a 95 on my math test, but all I can focus on is that my game got cancelled for tonight.

Color: Purple

I feel anxious and scared about changing schools. That means that the new school is going to be awful.

Color: Green

I bet when my parents get divorced, I will never see my dad, and everything in my life will change for the worse.

Color: Blue

Darnell needed to cancel our plans. I'm sure it's because he really doesn't like me.

Color: Yellow

My dad did something really bad and might go to jail. There is nothing good about him.

Color: Orange

It's raining outside. I'm sure it's going to be a terrible storm, and we will all get hurt.

Color: Red

STRENGTHEN IT

Do any of the thinking traps in the box above sound familiar? Put your top three thinking traps in the mouse traps below. These are the thinking traps that you tend to fall into most. Be on the lookout for your thinking traps when you feel a strong negative emotion. Don't get stuck!

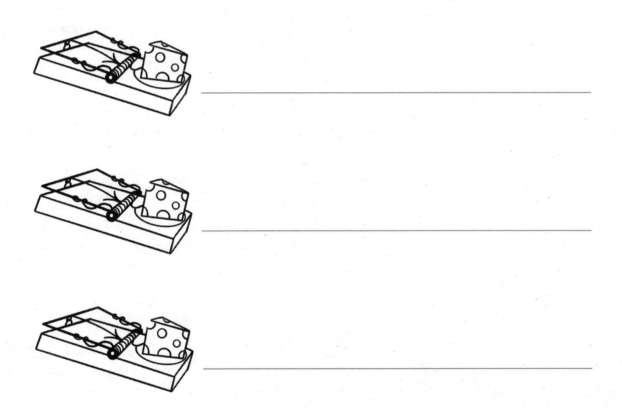

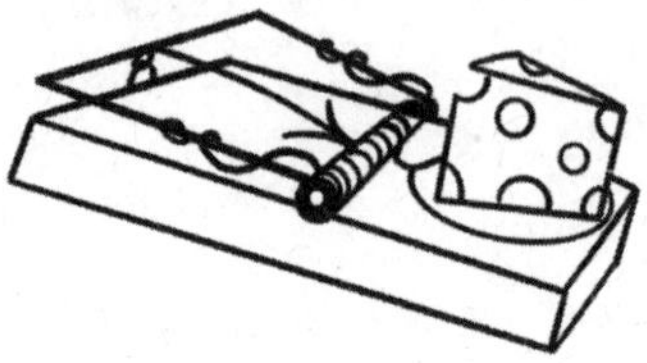

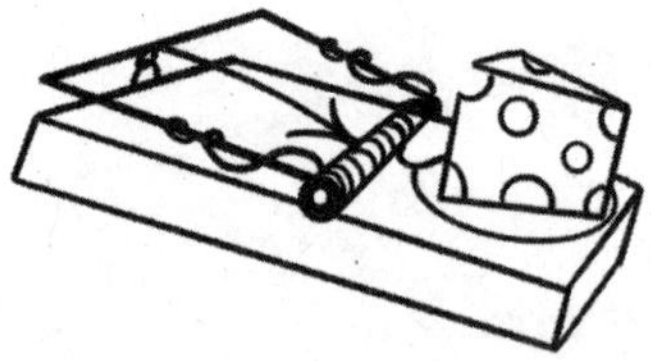

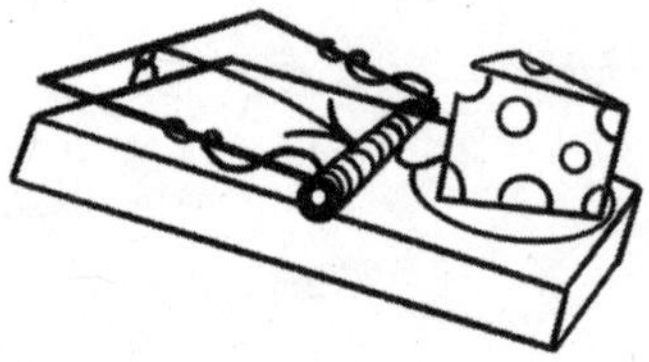

BONUS

(Do this one with your special adult.)

In this activity, you'll learn about a special skill you can use with sad or bad thoughts. It's called the three C's: catch it, check it, and change it.

With your special adult, share a time when you felt a strong negative emotion. Then use the strong emotion to catch the negative thought, check on it, and then change it so you can keep swimming.

1. **Catch it.** Imagine your thoughts are fish floating by in a stream. Catch the negative thought in your fishing net!

2. **Check it.** Look closely at the thought. Ask yourself: Does this thought help me, or just make me feel worse when I focus on it?

3. **Change it.** Substitute the negative thought with something positive.

Let's keep practicing the three C's. We've given you an example to help you start.

What happened?	Catch it: What did you think?	Check it: Is it helpful?	Change it: What is a helpful and true thought?
My dad is sick.	He's going to die.	Not helpful. This way of thinking is not going to cure my dad, and it is just going to make me more upset.	The doctor's taking care of my dad. He's a good doctor. Right now, let's take it one day at a time.

ACTIVITY 15

Challenging Your Negative Thoughts

LEARN IT

In the last activity, you identified your thinking traps and started to catch, check, and change them. In this activity, we'll give you some more tools to challenge unhelpful thinking patterns.

When you feel like you might be falling into a thinking trap, it can be helpful to ask yourself these three questions.

1. **What's the evidence** to support my thinking? Ask yourself, Is my thought a fact or a fiction? A fact is always true and based on evidence. An example of a fact is that Abraham Lincoln was our sixteenth president. A fiction is a made-up story like *Goldilocks and the Three Bears.* It's a nice story, but it's not true because it didn't really happen.

2. **Is it helpful?** Does the way I'm thinking make me feel better, or does it make me feel worse?

3. **What would I say to a friend** who was going through this situation? We're often nicer to our friends than to ourselves.

Once you ask yourself these questions, you can start to develop new ways of thinking that are more positive and realistic. Let's start challenging the make-believe stories we all have in our heads.

DO IT

Think about a difficult situation you've been in recently. Then, follow these steps to challenge your thoughts. This is the first step in figuring out what you want to *do* about the situation.

Step 1. Write down a stressful situation.

Step 2. Write down the negative emotion you experienced.

Step 3. Indicate your negative thoughts that caused that negative emotion.

Step 4. Challenge your thoughts by asking yourself:

- What is the evidence?

- Is the way I'm thinking helpful?

- What would I say to a friend in the same situation?

Step 5. Write down your new neutral or positive thoughts.

Step 6. Write down your new positive emotion(s).

Now you try. Use the chart on the next page to work through the process. An example has been given to start you off. There are also extra boxes so you can fill this out several times over the next few weeks. And if you'd like to practice more, you can download copies of this chart at http://www.newharbinger.com/49166. Ask an adult for help with that if you need it.

Situation	Negative Emotion(s)	Negative Thought(s)	What Is the Evidence?	Is It Helpful?	What Would I Say to a Friend?	Neutral or Positive Thought(s)	Positive Emotion(s)
I'm not in class with any of my friends.	Hopeless, lonely, and angry	I hate all the kids in my class. It's going to be a terrible year.	There isn't evidence it will be terrible. It's possible that I will meet new kids. And I can still hang out with my old friends out-side of class.	Not helpful. Thinking this way will make me angry, which isn't helpful if I want to meet new kids.	This is hard. However, it's an opportunity to meet new kids.	I will miss my friends, and this is also a chance to widen my friend group.	Calm. And a little bit excited.

STRENGTHEN IT

First, write a letter about a challenging situation you've faced. Include your thoughts and feelings, as it was happening to you. Use the words "my" and "I" in your letter.

> For example, **My parents are getting divorced. What's going to happen to me? Maybe it's my fault. It's going to be terrible. I am so upset.**

Your turn. (Remember to use "I" and "my" and purposely fall into many thinking traps.)

Now, write the same letter, but pretend you are writing it to a friend who is going through the same thing. Often, when you write the letter as if it were directed to a friend, it's easier to notice your own thinking traps, reduce upsetting emotions, and cope with difficult situations.

Here's an example of a letter Rebecca would've written to herself when she found out her parents were getting divorced. Notice that she uses her name and "you" even though she's talking about herself.

Dear Rebecca,

I know you're scared about your parents getting divorced. They still both love you, and it's not your fault. Things may be hard, and you may feel sad at times. It will get better. There are people who can help you, so you don't have to go through this alone.

Now you try. (Use your name and "you" in this letter.)

Did you notice that writing to yourself as if you were writing to a friend made you feel better? It's an excellent strategy to try when you are struggling with something difficult.

BONUS

(Do this one with your special adult.)

With your trusted adult, take a moment and think about a situation that is difficult for you. Together with your special adult, complete the following.

Write down a stressful situation you're worried about.

What's the *best thing* that could happen?

What's the *worst thing* that could happen?

What's the *most likely* thing to happen? (Hint: It might be something between the best and the worst thing.)

If you're like most kids, you'll see that your best and worst are improbable (not likely to happen). In contrast, what's probably going to occur is your "most likely" scenario.

Speaking of "likely," here's one last question to ask yourself and your trusted adult: Is the situation you are facing a **possibility or a probability**?

A *possibility* means it's possible, but unlikely to happen. For example, it's a possibility that it would snow in the summer in New York. But it's a really small one. It doesn't really snow in the summer all that much.

Meanwhile, a *probability* means there is a good chance or it's likely that something will happen. For example, if it is cloudy and gray outside, there is a good probability that it will rain.

If your situation is a probability, you should be concerned. However, if it is a possibility, you might've fallen into a thinking trap, and you need to get out.

ACTIVITY 16

Building Optimism

LEARN IT

Let's spend a little more time on one particular thinking trap—pessimism—and its opposite, optimism.

Pessimism is the tendency to see the worst in things or believe that the worst will happen. Pessimism is a key element in all the other types of thinking traps you've learned; it's what they all have in common.

The opposite of pessimism is optimism. Optimism is defined as the tendency to look on the bright side of events. It's the belief that good ultimately wins over bad—or that even when bad things happen, there are good things you can find and hold on to.

Research shows that people who are more optimistic are happier and more successful. Although it's true that some people are naturally more optimistic or pessimistic than others, you can always learn to be more optimistic.

Caren's mother is a great example of an optimist. She sees the good in every situation. Once when she was babysitting Caren's children, she and the kids got locked out of the house. It was getting dark, but Caren's mother made it an "adventure" by turning the search for the keys into a scavenger hunt under the stars.

People with a pessimistic attitude think that failure is personal, is terrible, and will happen again. If Caren's mother had been a pessimist, she might have panicked and felt like a bad person for losing the keys. And she might have decided she won't babysit in the future because she believes that she'll lose the keys again.

Pessimistic people engage in the "problematic P's": they think that bad things are personal, pervasive, and permanent. These are big words, but stick with us, and we'll explain them.

Personal. Pessimists believe that bad events are *all about them* and not the situation.

Pervasive. Pessimists believe that bad events are *enormous and impact every part of their lives.* These events feel like elephant and not ant problems.

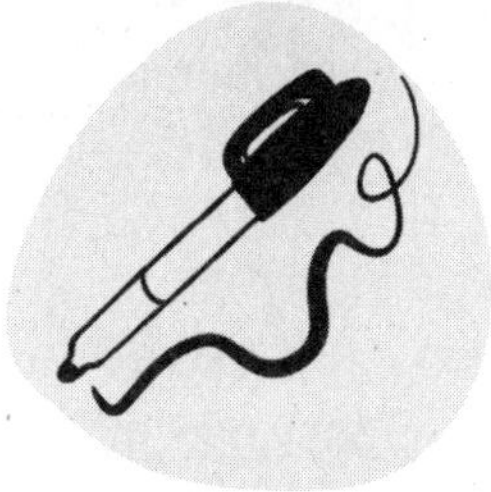

Permanent. Pessimists believe that bad events *will never change and last forever.*

Optimists, on the other hand, are less likely to fall into these traps. But optimism is not always being happy or blaming others when things go wrong. And optimism is not about pretending problems aren't problems or never having negative feelings, like sadness or anger.

What we are encouraging you to do is to be an "accurate optimist." An accurate optimist doesn't deny things that are hard. But they do look for the opportunities in all situations. And they look for the good in people and in themselves.

DO IT

Read each situation. Decide what an optimist would say and what a pessimist would say. Then, in the pessimistic thinking section, see if there is a problematic P in what you wrote. Look at the example below to help you.

Situation: Your teacher tells you the class will have indoor recess.	
Optimistic Thinking	Pessimistic Thinking
Indoor recess means I can play Uno. I haven't played it in a while. That game is fun!	The whole day stinks. Indoor recess is never fun! (Problematic P's: permanent and pervasive)

Now you try! For the situations below, write an optimistic and a pessimistic response. Feel free to include the specific problematic P you used.

Situation: You are struggling in math class.	
Optimistic Thinking	Pessimistic Thinking

Situation: Your best friend stops talking to you.	
Optimistic Thinking	Pessimistic Thinking

Situation: There is a hurricane on its way. The town is expected to lose power, and you've had to evacuate quickly until the storm passes. (Hint: This one is hard! Keep in mind that your goal here is to be an "accurate optimist": someone who looks for the good in a situation without ignoring what might make it hard.)	
Optimistic Thinking	Pessimistic Thinking

Once you've completed the exercise, consider which style of thinking was easier for you. In general, do you consider yourself more of an optimist or a pessimist? Circle one.

Optimist   Pessimist

If you're more often a pessimist, or you tend to be really pessimistic in certain situations, are there ways you can look for more of the problematic P's in your thinking so you can build your resilience? The next exercise will help.

STRENGTHEN IT

1. Think about a recent challenge where you engaged in pessimistic thinking. Write down the challenge.

____

2. Did you notice a problematic P?

   Did you make it personal (about you)?

   ____

   Did you make it pervasive (enormous)?

   ____

   Did you make it permanent (lasting forever)?

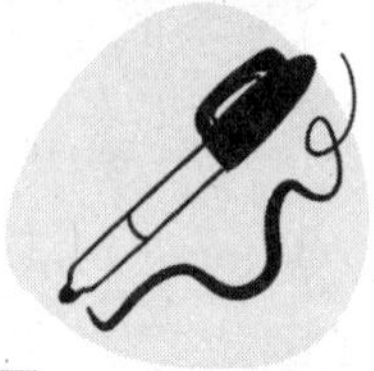

   ____

3. Thinking about that same challenge, can you have more optimistic thinking?

   Can you make it about the situation and not about you?

   ____

   Can you make it small (an ant problem)?

   ____

   Can you make it temporary (in the moment)?

   ____

BONUS

(Do this one with your special adult.)

When something happens that can be perceived as bad, try to find the good. Or, as Caren's mother would say, "Turn it into an adventure."

Think about a challenge or stressful situation you've faced. How might you see it in a more optimistic light or as an adventure?

Draw a picture of the adventure you described above. Show it to your special adult.

ACTIVITY 17

Growing a Growth Mindset

LEARN IT

Whether we respond to stressful times with resilience doesn't depend on just the individual thoughts we think. It also depends on the way we think in general: the kind of mindset we have. The type of mindset we're talking about is called having a *growth mindset.*

Having a growth mindset is about believing that your brain can grow when you work hard, find effective ways to deal with problems you face, and ask for support when you need it.

The opposite of a growth mindset is a *fixed mindset.* You believe that your abilities and brain are "fixed" and cannot change—that you're born smart, talented, patient, or determined or you're not. And often, you interpret going through a challenge or setback as evidence that you don't have what it takes. This way of thinking makes you more overwhelmed when you're facing a challenge or a setback. It also makes it easier to give up when you are struggling.

Recent research has found that growing a growth mindset should not only fall on you. The adults (teachers, parents, community members) and environment you're in need to believe in and encourage a growth mindset for you to receive the greatest impact from having a growth mindset. However you develop it, a growth mindset allows you to take on difficult things and to see challenges as opportunities to become better at certain skills. It also helps you cope with disappointments along the way. With a growth mindset, you won't see the obstacles you face as evidence that you aren't good or smart enough. You'll see them as opportunities to use your skills as a person—like your determination, creativity, and patience—and grow stronger.

DO IT

Below are some growth and fixed mindset statements. Put a circle around the growth mindset statements. Cross out the fixed mindset statements. Then check your answers at the end of this activity.

1. *I love challenges.*
2. *I am going to quit if I don't do well.*
3. *I can learn from my mistakes.*
4. *I like to try new things.*
5. *If you are smart, you don't have to try.*
6. *I hate it when my classmates do better than me.*
7. *I don't want to get just easy work. Hard work makes my brain bigger and stronger.*
8. *I am going to stay in the easy class so everyone will think I'm smart.*

When looking at these statements, did you feel more of a connection to the growth or fixed mindset statements?

Don't worry if you relate more to the fixed mindset statements. All of us deal with fixed mindsets in some way. And learning about your mindset, what you're doing right now, is growing and changing your brain. You're getting more of a growth mindset right now!

Answer Key: Statements 1, 3, 4, and 7 are growth mindset statements. Statements 2, 5, 6, and 8 are fixed mindset statements.

STRENGTHEN IT

We often have a growth mindset in one area and a fixed mindset in another. For example, you might have a growth mindset when you play sports but a fixed mindset when it comes to making friends.

It is important to know which areas you display a fixed mindset in and plan for them. It can even be helpful to talk to your inner fixed mindset when it shows up. Maybe even give it a name, like Mr. Fixie. It's also important to know where you have a growth mindset already. This will teach you how to deal with your fixed mindset when it shows up.

Write a letter to yourself about a time you used a growth mindset to build resilience. (Remember to use your name and the word "you" in your letter, even though you're talking to yourself.) If your fixed mindset emerged in the story you're telling, recognize it and call it out—give it a name.

Here's an example.

Dear Christina,

You have shown a growth mindset with reading. You have challenged yourself by reading challenging books and using different strategies to understand what you read. However, like most people, you don't have a growth mindset in everything. You can have a fixed mindset when it comes to math. When it comes to math, you often think you are either smart or you are not. From now on, every time Mr. Fixie pops up about math, remind yourself that everyone has things they are better and worse at. Keep practicing those hard math problems, use different strategies, and learn from your mistakes. You can also get help from others. You got this!

Now, you try.

Change takes time. But the next time you're in a situation where your fixed mindset shows up, see if you can tell yourself the same kinds of things you just said in your letter. It'll probably help!

ACTIVITY 18

The Power of "And" and "Yet"

LEARN IT

Did you know that there are two three-letter words that are powerful enough to change your mindset? What are these words? They are "and" and "yet." The words "and" and "yet" can allow you to be more accepting of all your feelings. And they can change your mindset from a fixed one to a growth one. Often, they'll remind you that change is possible and that the things you go through in life aren't set in stone. Let's look at each word individually.

You may be wondering, *How can "and" build resilience?* Using "and" lets you hold onto two truths, even if they seem like opposites. For example, "I am scared to get a strep test, *and* I will get the test because it is the safe thing to do."

Here's a tip: Whenever you're about to say "but," replace it with "and." It can be hard to do at first, but—no, wait—*and* with practice, you can do it!

The problem with the word "but" is that everything you say before the "but" gets lost or kicked to the curb. When you use "and," you remind yourself that both ideas are true. Let's look at the differences between "but" and "and."

You did well in soccer, BUT next time move a little quicker.

You did well in soccer, AND next time move a little quicker.

Using "and" lets you hold onto both ideas. Here's one more example.

I am excited BUT scared.

I am excited AND scared.

Can you see how using "and" in your thinking allows you to be more accepting and able to manage your emotions?

DO IT

Kick "but" to the curb when you talk to yourself or others. In the sentences below, cross out "but" and replace it with "and."

1. I am scared to go to school, but I will go anyway.
2. You showed good effort in class, but you need to come to extra help.
3. I am upset about moving, but I will have my own room in the new house.

Now let's learn about our other favorite three-letter-word: "yet."

LEARN IT

When looking at other people, it's easy to think that their journey has been easy, with no bumps along the way. However, if you look at anyone who has been successful, you'll find that there were many challenges and things that didn't come easily. Often, there are things that these people would one day be good at; however, they're just not there—*yet*.

If you add the word "yet" to your vocabulary, you acknowledge that you are a "work in progress." For example, maybe right now you can't shoot a three-pointer in basketball, solve a difficult math problem, or deal emotionally when your parents fight. See if you can add the word "yet" to those statements. It might encourage you to be more optimistic and have a growth mindset. Having a "yet" mindset also allows you to persist and to see mistakes as a "first attempt in learning" (FAIL) rather than an end point.

But getting to "yet" is not easy. If you are faced with a challenge, a tough situation, or a setback, it is sometimes easier to just say, "I can't." So how can you get to "yet"?

1. First, take a deep breath to help you think more clearly.
2. Focus on why the challenge you're facing is important to you.
3. View the challenge as an essential part of the process of getting through this situation, rather than as evidence you should quit.
4. Ask for support to help you get through the difficulty you're dealing with.

It is important to note that it is not always possible to reach "yet" in all situations. Maybe that three-pointer is just too hard to make right now. And in those instances, the wisest choice may be to change your expectations. For example, if you don't make the basketball team this year, you can join the kids you see playing a friendly game every afternoon. You'll be able to enjoy yourself—and maybe even improve your game so you can try again next year. Being ready to sometimes adopt more realistic expectations or figuring out a new path toward the same goal is also being resilient.

STRENGTHEN IT

Now, let's practice using "yet." Every time you hear a voice in your head saying, "I am not," or "I can't ______________________," add YET. For example, "I am not good at fractions…YET!" Or, "I can't write in cursive…YET!"

Now you try with something you need to be more resilient with, in an area such as school, family, home, activities, feelings, or whatever it is. First, use "yet" to expand your thinking. Then, try to figure out some ways to practice the skill or behavior you want to improve on.

Write down something you can't do...YET!

____

Write down the strategies on the steps of the ladder to turn your "can't yet" into a "can."

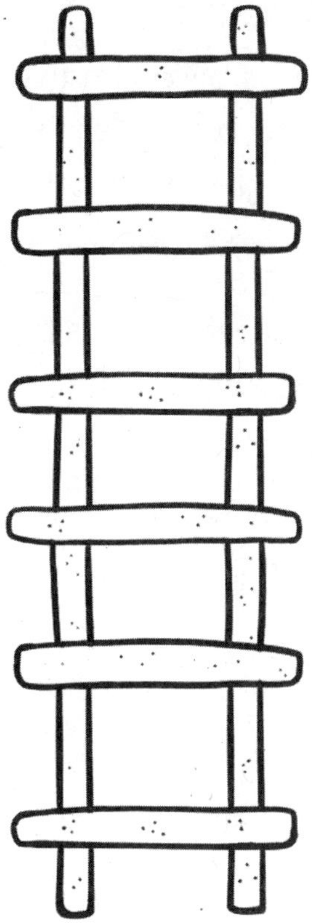

ACTIVITY 19

Tapping into What's Important

LEARN IT

It's hard to go through stressful times. Even when you accept your feelings, challenge your negative thoughts, and incorporate the words "yet" and "and" into your vocabulary, it can be difficult to manage life's ups and downs.

One of the best strategies when you feel really stuck is to think about what is most important to you, or your *values*. Values are things that you want your life to be about, like family, kindness, or courage.

Values act like a compass on your ship. They help you make choices based on the direction you want your life to go. When you connect and tap into your values, you can do the things that are meaningful to you, even in the face of difficult or painful experiences, which builds resilience.

Keep in mind that values are not what others expect of you. Every person gets to choose their own values. Let's start thinking about the values that are important to you.

DO IT

Read the following values. Which ones are most important to you? Which ones do you like in yourself? If another value that's not in this list comes to mind, write it down below. This activity requires some deep thinking. It's okay to get some support from a trusted adult if you get stuck.

Achievement	Faith	Learning
Adventure	Family	Loyalty
Courage	Independence	Peace
Caring	Fun	Responsibility
Community	Happiness	Wisdom
Curiosity	Health	______________
Creativity	Honesty	______________
Fairness	Humor	______________
Friendship	Leadership	______________

STRENGTHEN IT

Choose your top three values and rank them below.

1. ______________________________

2. ______________________________

3. ______________________________

Now, write about one of your top three values that you selected from above. Try to answer the following questions: What does this value mean to me? Why is this value important? How did I learn this value? How can I use this value to help me accomplish my goals and face hard things? How does this value make me stronger and more resilient?

Need some help? Check out Caren's example. Notice how Caren uses her own name, "she," and "her" in the example below.

> Caren has a value of caring. She learned this value from watching her parents. When hard things happen, she cares for others, which helps her feel useful and not alone in having struggles. This allows her to be more resilient.

Now you try.

____

____

____

____

____

____

Connecting to your values helps you cope better with stress. In the space below write words or pictures of your top values. Keep this reminder in a place where you can see it every day. This way your values are front and center: it's clear to you what makes your challenge worth going through.

BONUS

(Do this one with your special adult.)

Ask your special adult about their values. Are they similar to yours? Ask your special adult to share a story about a time they used their values to meet a challenge. How does your special adult use their values to be more resilient?

ACTIVITY 20

Hope and "Failing Forward"

LEARN IT

Hope is defined as having both the will and the way to achieve what you want.

Will	+	Way	=	Hope
(motivation)		(plan of action)		

Some people are naturally more hopeful, but like the other skills we have talked about, you can grow hope with practice. Here are some ways.

- Try to focus more on your strengths and solutions rather than the "problem." For example, if someone tells you they don't want to be your friend anymore, instead of getting stuck on that (the problem), you might try to use your sense of humor (a strength) to make new friends (a solution).
- Practice optimism by looking for the good even in difficult situations. This doesn't mean denying that something is hard and painful. But it does mean looking for the positives you can find, even if you would never have chosen the experience.
- When you face obstacles, make a plan for dealing with them, as best you can. For example, say you're feeling a lot of grief when your pet dies. When you notice this feeling, figure out steps you can take to deal with what you feel and feel better. For example, you might talk to your special adult. Or, you might have a ceremony to honor your pet.

- Recognize that no one experiences life without some challenges and setbacks. Remind yourself that when you see someone else's success, it's like an iceberg. It looks strong and perfect on top, but what you don't see is what's underneath. Underneath is all the messy stuff: setbacks, failures, and hard work. Remember there is always a messy part. We just don't always see it.

So, when you face a challenge or setback, take a deep breath, acknowledge the yuck, and remind yourself that this is the messy part of the iceberg. And ask yourself, When I fail, can I "fail forward" so I learn, grow, and become stronger? And remember, you can try to get support when meeting challenges. Having support from others is often the antidote, or the secret weapon, against stress.

DO IT

Write out a FAIL (first attempt in learning) and what you learned on the brick wall on the following page. We have contributed a few FAILs to start you off.

Caren's FAIL: I lost my car keys when I was hiking with my dog in the woods. I needed to be rescued by my husband. What I Learned: Wear pants with a zipped pocket when going hiking.	Rebecca's FAIL: I wore two different shoes to work! What I Learned: I learned it's important to keep my shoes more organized and to laugh at myself because everyone makes mistakes.

What about you—what's a FAIL you've had in the past?

____

____

And what did you learn from it?

____

____

____

After you complete your own FAIL, talk to someone you admire and ask them to share a FAIL they once had. Caren did this activity in her school, and people wrote back to her students with interesting FAILs.

Then, add your FAIL, plus others, to the FAIL wall on the next page.

By being public with our failures, we help each other see that failure is a natural part of the process, and we don't feel so alone.

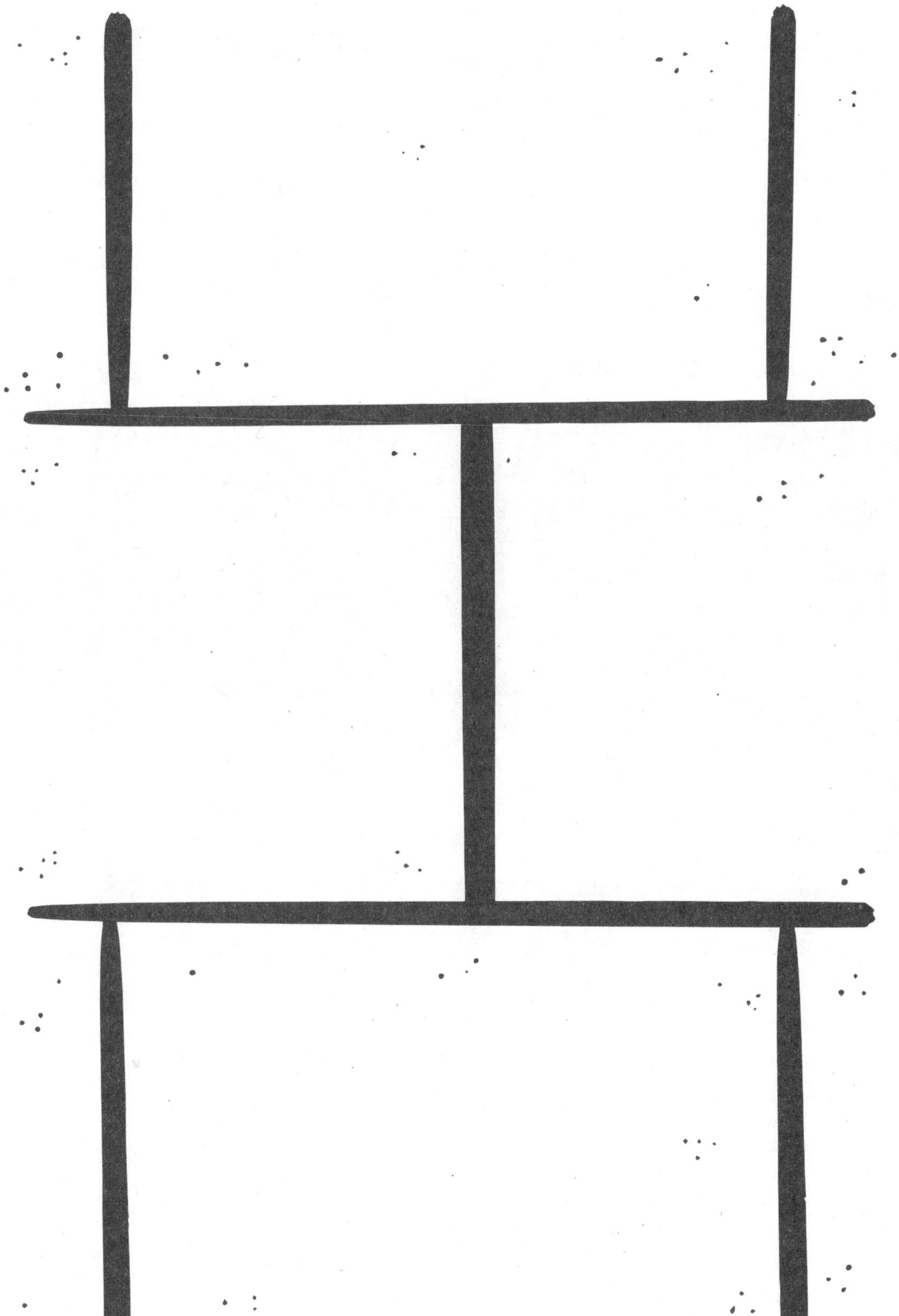

STRENGTHEN IT

Although we can learn from failures, recent research tells us that for lots of kids, thinking about success helps them achieve more. Can you imagine a bright, happy future for yourself? In this future, you have overcome your obstacles, you achieved your goals, and everything has gone as well as possible.

Draw a picture below of what that would look like. Put in lots of details. Where are you? How did you get there? What obstacles did you face? Who helped you along the way?

Talk about your drawing with your special adult.

Did drawing your picture give you hope? We hope so!

RESILIENCE CHECKPOINT

You made it to your third checkpoint. Here's a quick summary of what we hope you've learned about resilient thinking:

- How your thoughts, feelings, and actions are connected
- What your personal thinking traps are
- How to challenge unhelpful thinking
- Ways to build optimism and a growth mindset
- How to tap into what is important to you, or your values
- How to see obstacles as opportunities to grow and to "fail forward"

Let's check your learning a little more.

Read the statements below and decide if each statement is a *fact* (true) or a *fiction* (false). Mark each one, and then check your answers in the key underneath.

1. "But" is a three-letter word that can help you build your resilience. FACT FICTION
2. The three problematic P's are personal, pervasive, and permanent. FACT FICTION
3. A thought is not a fact. FACT FICTION
4. Believing that your brain grows through hard work, strategies, and effort is called having a fixed mindset. FACT FICTION
5. Optimism is the tendency to look on the bright side of events. FACT FICTION

Answers: 1. Fiction. "And" and "yet" are the three-letter words that build resilience. 2. Fact. 3. Fact. 4. Fiction. Believing that your brain can grow through hard work, use of effective strategies, and effort is called a growth mindset. 5. Fact.

CROSSWORD PUZZLE

This puzzle incorporates all the vocabulary used in part 3. If you get stuck, remember to use your resilient mindset and get help from your special adult. (You can also find the answers in the Answer Key at the end of the book if you want to check your work.)

ACROSS

4 It's the truth (4)

5 Alternative to brain (6)

8 Japanese fish dish (5)

9 Float in a boat (4)

10 Being active (5)

12 Anger (3)

13 What one with 17D has (4)

15 Clear (3)

16 "Can-do" attitude (6, 7)

19 So far (3)

20 Accomplished (4)

21 Little troublemaker (3)

22 What you believe in (6)

23 Use your head (5)

24 All the time (9)

27 What's on the clock (4)

28 Ought to (6)

29 Had dinner (3)

DOWN

1 Requests help (4)

2 Negative attitude (9)

3 "Absolutely!" (3)

4 Emotion (7)

6 "Can't-do" attitude (5, 7)

7 Long (for) (4)

9 "Get the picture?" (3)

11 Thankfulness (9)

14 Reasons (8)

17 Looking on the bright side (8)

18 Don't fall in here (4)

19 Kind of tent (4)

22 Energy (3)

25 "Go on..." (3)

26 Safety feature (3)

Get ready to put those thoughts into action and learn about resilient behavior. Ready, set, go!

PART 4

Resilient Actions: Ready, Set, Go!

"You can't be that kid standing at the top of the waterslide, overthinking it. You have to go down the chute."

—Tina Fey

WHAT YOU'LL DISCOVER

In part 2, you learned all about feelings. In part 3, you learned all about thinking. But there is still one point of our triangle-shaped sail from activity 13 we haven't covered yet: doing, or actions. That's what part 4 is all about: how to build resilient behaviors through your actions.

In part 4, you will:

- Learn to build "I can do it" muscles through confidence, control, and competence.
- Practice hard things to build bravery.
- Develop coping and problem-solving skills.
- Learn to be flexible.
- Grow your strengths.
- Take care of yourself.

So let's get busy "doing" resilient behaviors!

ACTIVITY 21

Building "I Can Do It" Muscles

LEARN IT

A great place to start developing resilient behaviors is by building "I can do it" muscles, or what scientists call self-efficacy [self-eff-ick-us-ee]. Self-efficacy is believing in your ability to solve a problem or perform a task. It's built when you do hard things and master them. An excellent example of a character who showed self-efficacy is the little engine from the story *The Little Engine That Could.* The Little Engine succeeded by showing *confidence* by believing she could get the job done. She focused on what she could *control* (pulling the train full of goodies). And, by accomplishing her task, she gained a sense of *competence*, declaring, "I knew I could!"

So how can you be like the little engine and build your "I can do it" muscles? Here are three ways.

Build your confidence. Lots of kids think, *I have to feel confident before I can take on a challenge.* However, it's actually the reverse. When you try hard things and succeed, you build confidence. Think of something that scares you a little bit. Then, ask yourself: What baby steps can I take to get stronger? What kinds of things have I done in the past that have helped me succeed? Remembering how you were successful in the past builds confidence in your ability to succeed in the future.

Focus on what you can control. In life, there are things you can control and things you can't. Resilient people focus on what they can control and let go of the rest. By focusing on what you can control, you will feel more confident and in charge of your life—all building blocks to developing resilience.

Gain a sense of competence. "Competence" is a fancy word for the ability to do something successfully. It's the feeling you get after you succeed at something, like tying your shoes or riding a bike. You feel competent after you have mastered something tough. And you feel inspired to face future challenges with more confidence and strength.

DO IT

Think about a time when you were like the Little Engine. What was the challenge you faced? For example, maybe you broke your leg and had to figure out how to deal with that. Or maybe you tried to do something new and really struggled for a while.

Think about what you have done in the past that helped. Past success builds future success and confidence. For example, if you broke your leg, maybe you asked your friends to carry your books. Or, if you were trying to learn something new, maybe you talked to someone who could help you.

Think about the parts of the situation that you couldn't control. For example, if you broke your leg, you can't really control that.

I couldn't control: ____

____

Now think about the parts of the situation you could control. For example, if you broke your leg, you could get help carrying your stuff.

I could control: ____

____

Write a list of things you did to make the situation better. For example, maybe when you got hurt, you invited your friends over to sign your cast. It made you feel better to remember that they care. You feel more competent because you have a plan and support.

What I did: ____

____

____

I felt more competent because: ____

____

____

____

____

STRENGTHEN IT

Think about a stressful situation you are facing or one you have faced. In the outer circle, write the parts you can't control. In the inner circle, list the things you can control. For example, the broken leg part would go in the outer circle. The friends helping and signing your cast would go in the inner circle.

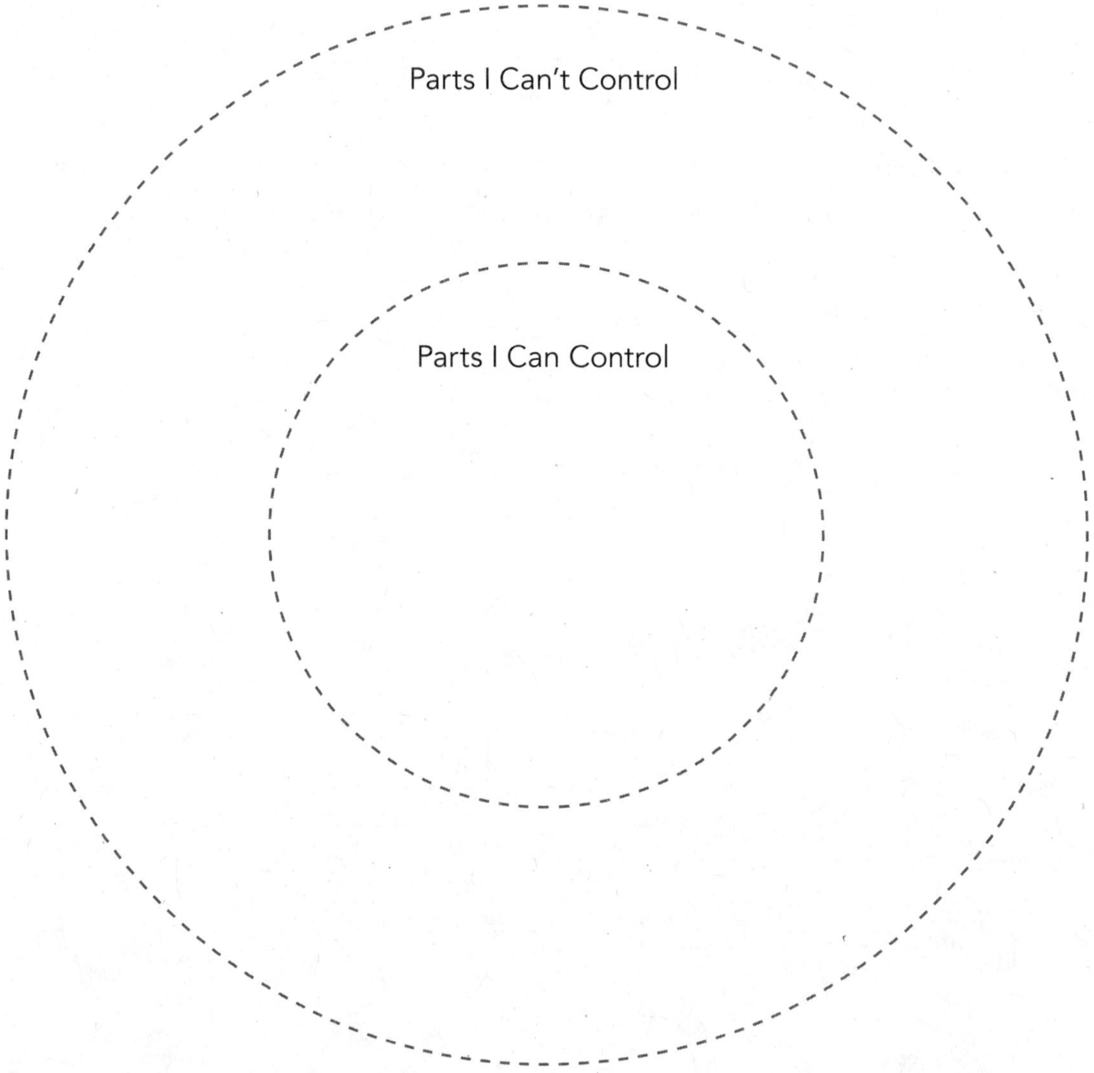

See if you can focus on the inner circle and let go of the rest.

ACTIVITY 22

Being Brave

LEARN IT

Lots of people think bravery means never feeling afraid. It's easy to think that because from the outside, brave people often look impressive, powerful, and sure of themselves. However, true bravery means feeling scared and uncertain *and* doing it anyway.

Learning to be brave isn't about learning a trick to make you not scared. It's about understanding that it's okay to feel scared, worried, or doubtful and still do the best you can.

Sometimes you only have to feel brave for a few seconds at a time—just long enough for you to face the fear. And when you start to take an action toward what you fear, you often find that it's not as bad as you thought.

So how do you demonstrate bravery?

- Avoid avoidance. It's natural to want to avoid what you fear, but the act of avoidance just reinforces that what you hear and see are super scary.
- Use the "I can do it" muscles we discussed in the previous activity.
- Break scary stuff down into manageable, bite-size steps. By taking on a challenge in this way, you will feel more competent.

- Act brave, and the brave feeling will come after. By *acting* brave, you will come to *feel* brave.
- Challenge your negative thoughts. Remind yourself that it's not the situation but how you *think* about the situation that affects how you feel.
- Get support. Having support allows you to accomplish more than you could do alone.

DO IT

In the space below, draw or write about a time you were brave. Make sure to include lots of details. The next time you're feeling scared, look at the picture you drew or the story you wrote. Remind yourself that you were brave and you can be brave again.

STRENGTHEN IT

To build bravery, it can help to take small, manageable steps. Imagine you were in the deep water trying to get onto a dock or a boat. It would be much easier to get out of the water if you had a ladder to help you. To see how this works, look at Rebecca's example of a time she was brave.

Rebecca's Bravery Ladder

I will be brave by: making new friends at my new school.

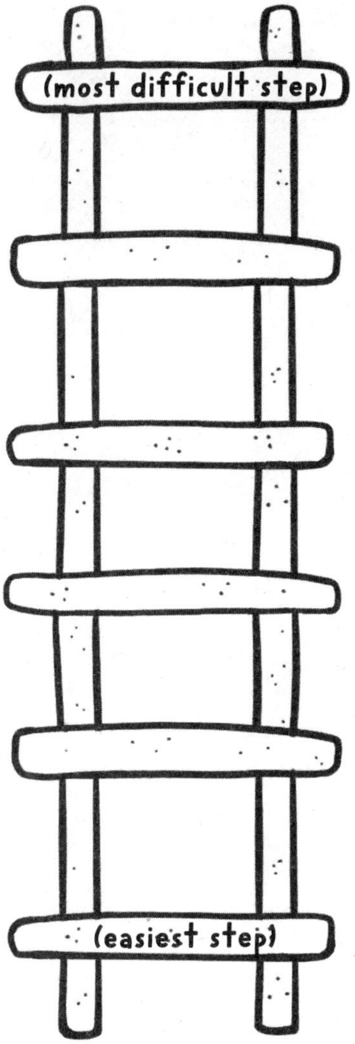

I will ask someone to exchange phone numbers.
(most difficult step)

I will ask kids at the lunch table some questions.

I will walk with a classmate to the lunchroom.

I will ask a classmate a question about the schoolwork.

I will say "hello" to kids I meet in my class.

I will smile at the kids from my new school.
(easiest step)

Now, it's your turn. At the very top of the ladder, write something that you need bravery to accomplish. Then, for each step of the ladder, write one small step you can do to face the fear. Each step will cause some level of fear (that's what bravery is all about). Start at the bottom, and once it feels easy, move up to the next step. You may need to repeat each step several times before it feels easy. By taking small steps, you will grow your confidence and be more willing to climb all the way up! Feel free to get some help from your special adult in completing this exercise.

I will be brave by: ______________________________

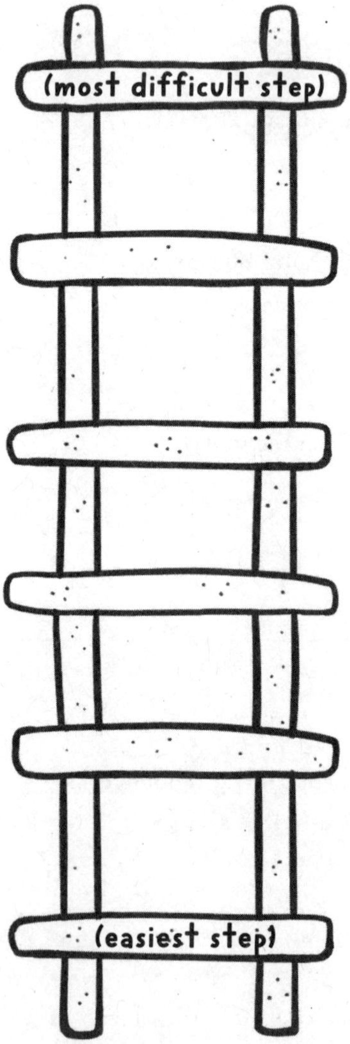

____

____

____

____

____

____

When you choose to be brave, you change yourself and the world in a positive way, one small courageous step at a time.

ACTIVITY 23

Coping with Hard Things

LEARN IT

Coping skills are tools you use to manage strong uncomfortable emotions and stress. When faced with a disappointment or an obstacle, you can use coping skills to help you feel safe, calm, and in control.

There are helpful coping skills, like taking a deep breath, talking to a grown-up, or drawing about your feelings. And there are unhelpful ways of coping, like avoiding hard things, yelling, or being physical. It's easy to fall back on unhelpful coping habits, so it's important to have a list of your go-to coping skills right at your fingertips. This way you can deal more effectively when you feel overwhelmed and respond in a way that you will be proud of.

Here's a way to help you cope. It's called the STOP skill.

Stop
Take a step back
Observe
Proceed mindfully

S. Stop. Don't do anything. Your emotions may want you to act without thinking, but you got this. Stay in control and stop!

T. Take a step back. Instead of going forward, take a deep breath and count to ten. Act responsively rather than reactively.

O. Observe. Notice what is happening inside and outside of your body. Do you notice your heart beating or your hands sweating? How are you thinking about the situation? What is going on around you?

P. Proceed mindfully. Act with awareness. Consider what will be best in the long run, not just what will help right now. Ask yourself, Will acting this way make the situation better or worse?

DO IT

When you are having a tough day or facing a challenge, choose a coping strategy from the treasure chest below. Ask yourself, Does it make me feel better? If not, choose another one. Feel free to add your own coping skills to the chest too.

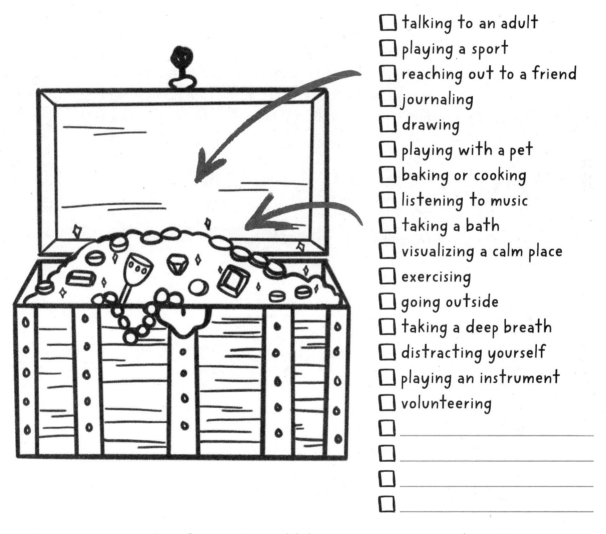

- [ ] talking to an adult
- [ ] playing a sport
- [ ] reaching out to a friend
- [ ] journaling
- [ ] drawing
- [ ] playing with a pet
- [ ] baking or cooking
- [ ] listening to music
- [ ] taking a bath
- [ ] visualizing a calm place
- [ ] exercising
- [ ] going outside
- [ ] taking a deep breath
- [ ] distracting yourself
- [ ] playing an instrument
- [ ] volunteering
- [ ] ____________________
- [ ] ____________________
- [ ] ____________________
- [ ] ____________________

As you grow your list of strategies, add them to your treasure chest. You can also print out your own copy of the treasure chest at http://www.newharbinger.com/49166 so you can post it somewhere you can easily see it. (Ask your special adult for help with this if you need it.)

STRENGTHEN IT

Some coping strategies work better than others depending on how upset you feel. Select a coping strategy from the list in the last section or one you added to the list. Then match your favorite coping skill to how upset you are by using the feeling thermometer as a guide. For example, if you feel like a 9 because your classmates tease you about your skin color or some other aspect of your appearance, you can use the coping strategy of talking with an adult. If you feel like a 5 because you did poorly on a test, planning to study better might be best in that situation. Keep the list handy so you can be reminded what coping strategy to use when you have an uncomfortable feeling.

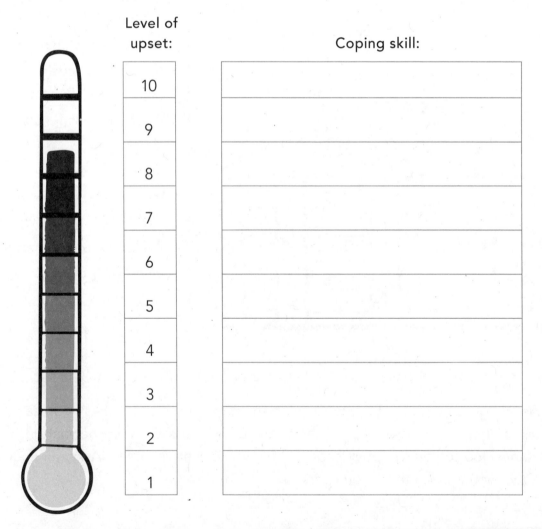

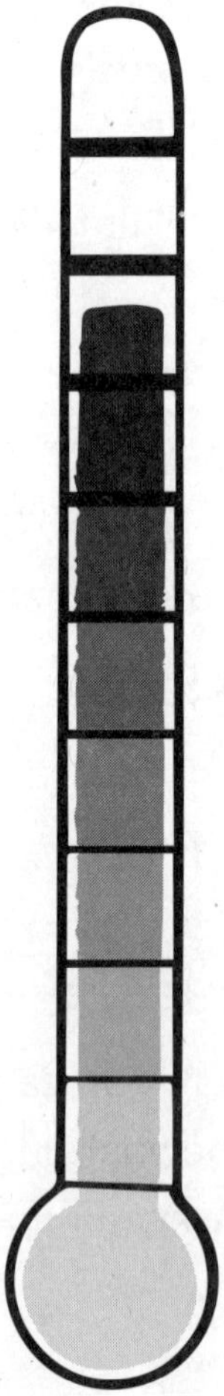

Level of upset:	Coping skill:
10	
9	
8	
7	
6	
5	
4	
3	
2	
1	

ACTIVITY 24

Solving Problems and Seeking Solutions

LEARN IT

It's easy when faced with a challenge to get stuck in the yuck. You can feel like there's no hope and no way out. You might want to keep talking about how mad, sad, or bad you feel. You may even get annoyed when someone wants to help you look at solutions. It's important to feel all your feelings, even the yucky ones, before you start seeking solutions, but then you have to decide. You can keep focusing on the problem, or you can choose to look for solutions.

It's like if you were in a boat that was filling with water. You could be angry that it was sinking, or you could find a way to get to safety.

We encourage you to move to safety by:

1. Defining the problem. Ask yourself, What is the problem I need to solve?
2. Noticing your feelings. Ask yourself, What am I feeling?
3. Focusing on what you can control.
4. Brainstorming ideas to create a plan to help.
5. Writing if-then sentences for each good option.
6. Picking the option with the best if-then chance.
7. Revising your plan. All plans need revisions.

DO IT

Let's practice the seven steps for problem solving and finding solutions. Look at our example and then try it yourself.

Define the problem.	Notice your feelings.	Focus on what you can control.	Brainstorm ideas to create a plan to help.	Write if-then sentences for each good option.	Pick the option with the best if-then chance.	Revise your plan.
There are really rough kids at the playground. It's not safe to go there.	I feel scared, angry, and frustrated.	I can't control what happens at the playground. I can control that I can play in other safe places.	I can play after school in the schoolyard. I can play in my yard or on my front stoop.	If I ask my mom if I can stay at school, then she will probably say yes. If I play in my yard or on my stoop, then I will have to play games that don't need a lot of space.	Staying after school would be my best option because I will have more space and friends to play with.	My mom works late on Tuesdays, so she can't pick me up late from school on that day. On Tuesdays, I will play in my yard.

Now you try. Think of a problem that you are struggling with. Apply the seven steps to that problem.

Define the problem.	Notice your feelings.	Focus on what you can control.	Brainstorm ideas to create a plan to help.	Write if-then sentences for each good option.	Pick the option with the best if-then chance.	Revise your plan.

STRENGTHEN IT

When faced with a challenge, there are often pros and cons that affect your decision making. Write down a challenge. Then weigh the pros and cons of your decision to determine the best solution. Below is an example.

The challenge: You tried out for the soccer team. You were told that you didn't make the team, but you could play with the team during practices.

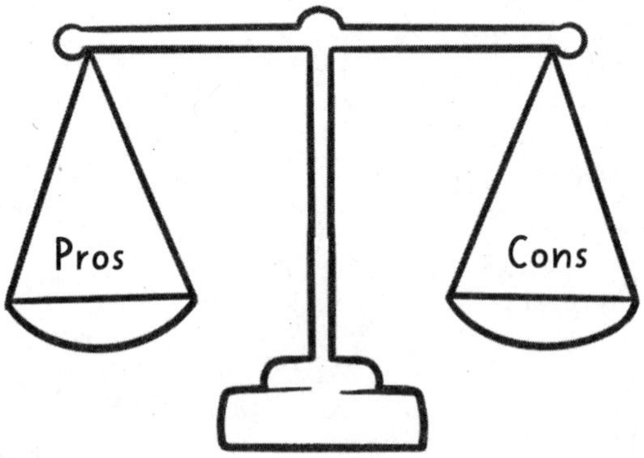

Pros:	Cons:
The pros of saying yes are that you get to practice your skills and hang out with your soccer friends.	The cons are you don't get to play during the games, and maybe it feels a little embarrassing.

After weighing your options, you decide to say yes.

Action I will take: I will say yes to joining the team.

Now it's your turn. Write down your challenge. Weigh the pros and cons to determine the best action you should take. Notice that there often isn't a best choice, just a better one. Also, keep in mind that the better choice will often serve you well in the long term, not just immediately. For example, not joining the team for practices may feel good immediately because it is less "embarrassing," but in the long run, it isn't the best because what you really want is to get better at soccer. Write out the action you will take on the bottom of the scale.

The challenge: ______________________________

____

Pros:	Cons:

Action I will take: ______________________________

____

____

____

ACTIVITY 25

Bending, Not Breaking

LEARN IT

Picture a sail on a boat. When the wind hits the sail, it bends to capture the wind and that moves the boat where it needs to go. The sail isn't rigid and stiff; if it was, it would break with the force of the wind. To be resilient, you need to be flexible like a sailor, adjusting your sail, making small turns in the right directions, and using the wind to get you where you want to go.

So how can you be like a sailor, building flexibility muscles as you go?

1. Define the problem.
2. Identify different ways of thinking about the problem.
3. Brainstorm many ways to solve the problem.
4. Be open or flexible to any of the solutions.
5. Remind yourself that life is full of curves; don't expect it to be a straight path.

Let's look at Kevin. He's struggling with being flexible. He wanted to play tag at recess and got upset when he learned that tag wasn't an option. Instead of being flexible and trying something new at recess, he sat on the sidelines, sulking and missing out on having fun.

It's okay to feel disappointed when plan A doesn't work, but it's resilient to say to yourself, "I can't stick with my original plan A, but the alphabet has twenty-five more letters! Time for plan B or C!" That's being flexible.

DO IT

To increase flexibility, it's good to be able to see many solutions. Try the exercise with Kevin's example from the last section.

Step 1. Write down the problem.

Step 2. Think of three possible ways to look at the problem.

Step 3. Brainstorm three different solutions to the problem.

The problem: ______________________________

Possible ways for Kevin to look at the problem:

1. ______________________________
2. ______________________________
3. ______________________________

Brainstorm three solutions:

1. ______________________________

2. ______________________________

3. ______________________________

Now try the same thing with a stressful situation you're facing.

The problem: ______________________________

Possible ways to look at the problem.

1. ______________________________

2. ______________________________

3. ______________________________

Brainstorm solutions:

1. ______________________________

2. ______________________________

3. ______________________________

STRENGTHEN IT

Here's a riddle: What are two things you find on a boat that can stop the boat from moving?

Hint: One is flexible, and one is inflexible.

______________________ ______________________

Write about a time you were flexible (like a rope) and a time you were inflexible (like an anchor).

I showed flexible behavior: ______________________

____

What helped me to be flexible was: ______________________

____

____

____

I demonstrated inflexible behavior: ______________________

____

What got in my way was: ______________________

____

____

____

Answer: rope and anchor

BONUS

(Do this one with your special adult.)

Ask your special adult to share times they demonstrated flexible and inflexible behavior. Ask your special adult, What made it easier and harder to be flexible?

ACTIVITY 26

Using Your Strengths

LEARN IT

Every superhero has a set of powers, and so do you. Your strengths are your superpowers. A strength is something you are naturally good at or that is important to you. Strengths are your positive qualities that help you achieve your goals.

To figure out what your strengths are, ask yourself the following questions: What do I love to do? What do I find easy to do or learn?

Here's a list of common strengths kids like you can have: love, kindness, creativity, curiosity, and humor. We added bravery and perseverance because these are necessary to build resilience.

DO IT

Mirror, mirror on the wall, what's my greatest strength of all? Write or draw a picture of you showing your top strength in the mirror below.

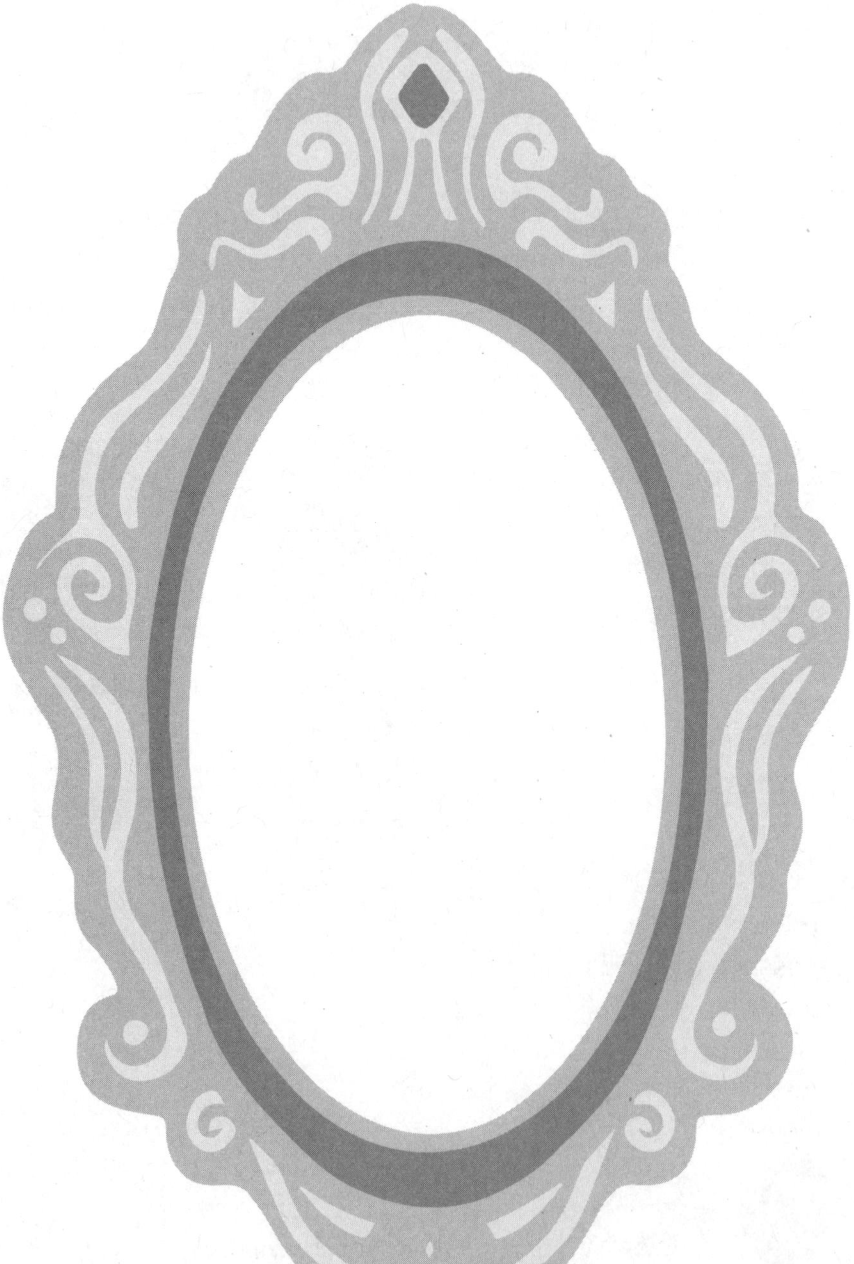

How can you use your strengths at home, at school, or in the community? How can you use your superpowers to grow your resilience? For example, if your superpower is humor, how can you use humor when you make a mistake or don't do as well as you would like?

STRENGTHEN IT

Draw a picture of yourself showing off one of your strengths. For example, if kindness is your strength, you can draw a picture of yourself doing an act of kindness. See if you can draw yourself using your strength in a way that helps not only yourself, but others too.

BONUS

(Do this one with your special adult.)

For this activity, you'll write a special kind of poem using the letters of your first name. It's called an acrostic poem. Each starting letter will represent a strength you have. Use a separate sheet of paper so you can hang your poem up somewhere afterwards. Have your special adult do one too! When you're done, display your poem in a place everybody can see.

Check out Caren's poem as an example.

C. Caring

A. Artistic

R. Reliable

E. Energetic

N. Nurturing

ACTIVITY 27

Taking Care of Yourself

LEARN IT

Self-care is anything that helps you take care of you. It's stuff like sleeping enough, exercising, and playing your musical instrument. Each of us is unique, so the kind of self-care that'll work best for each of us will be different too. And remember, self-care is not being selfish. It's essential to your well-being and builds resilience.

Sleep. Did you know that getting enough sleep improves your attention, memory, mood, and overall health? If you don't get enough sleep, you can feel stressed or grumpy. To sleep well, make sure the room you sleep in is dark and cozy. Light and noise can negatively affect your sleep. Shut off all devices at least an hour before bedtime. And try to stick to a regular bedtime and wake time. Just like you set an alarm to wake up, set an alarm to go to bed.

Good nutrition. Eating healthy helps your body stay strong. Our bodies are made up of 60 percent water, so we need to drink at least six to eight glasses of water a day to stay hydrated. It's best to eat lots of vegetables, fruits, and lean protein.

Exercise. Physical exercise is a natural stress-buster. It calms you down and relaxes you, because it uses up energy and gets rid of tension in a natural way. By exercising sometime during the day, you will feel better, sleep better at night, and be in a better mood. It is recommended that kids get sixty minutes of exercise every day. It can be walking, riding your bike, swimming, or any other activity that gets your body moving.

Play. Playing relaxes your brain and helps you connect with others. Play can be formal like a sport, or informal like imaginary play. One type of play is having a hobby. When Caren was little, she loved collecting puffy stickers with googly eyes. When Rebecca was your age, she loved riding her bike. If you don't have a hobby, think of one you might enjoy, like reading, collecting something, or cooking.

Engage in the arts and be creative. Using art for self-care can include creating art—whether it's temporary, like sandcastles or snowmen, or something like painting, drawing, and modeling clay. Creating rhythmic music can be particularly soothing. Drumming, singing, and listening to music with a steady beat are just a few examples of rhythmic music.

Meditation. Meditation is a powerful way to take care of yourself. Taking five slow, deep breaths while noticing how your body feels is a good way to be in the present moment. Remember we talked about mindfulness back in activity 11? You can try one of those activities now.

Nature. Scientists have discovered that looking at pictures of nature helps people to cope better with stress. And if looking at pictures decreases stress, imagine the power of actually walking in the forest, or going to the beach or local park. Combining exercise with nature builds resilience. Try taking a fifteen-minute "awe walk" where you appreciate the small wonders and beauty surrounding you. This can reduce stress and increase positive emotions.

Simple pleasures. Each and every day, do at least one activity that makes you happy. It can be coloring, riding your bike, or petting your dog. You can also review activity 9 for a reminder of how simple micro-moments of warm connection with others can improve your happiness, health, and resilience.

DO IT

Everyone needs different things, but we all can benefit from self-care. Try something from the list of self-care activities below. Did the activity make you feel better, the same, or worse? We left room for you to add your personal favorite self-care activity.

Self-Care Activity	How did it make you feel?		
Go for a walk	Better	Same	Worse
Read a book	Better	Same	Worse
Play an instrument	Better	Same	Worse
Take a nap	Better	Same	Worse
Play with a pet or stuffed animal	Better	Same	Worse
Take a bath or shower	Better	Same	Worse
Talk to a friend or family member	Better	Same	Worse
Listen to music	Better	Same	Worse
Get a hug	Better	Same	Worse
Watch a funny video	Better	Same	Worse
Cook or bake something	Better	Same	Worse
Write in a journal	Better	Same	Worse
Do some yoga	Better	Same	Worse
Color	Better	Same	Worse
Engage in a hobby Name it here: ____________________	Better	Same	Worse
____________________	Better	Same	Worse

STRENGTHEN IT

Take the self-care challenge. Fill in the following sentences. Then, challenge yourself to meet these goals in the next few weeks. If you find it difficult at first, it's okay. It may take time for you to get used to better self-care. But if you're patient and you persist, the benefits for your health and resilience will be worth it!

→ I will eat better by eating more ______________________________

and less ______________________________.

→ I will sleep ________ hours a night. I will ______________________________

______________________________ so I can sleep better.

→ I will get more exercise by ______________________________

______________ every day.

→ I will pick the following self-care activity ______________________________

______________________________.

I will do it every day.

BONUS

(Do this one with your special adult.)

Sometimes when you can't fall asleep, a good bedtime story can help. Here's one about a magical ship that involves all five senses. Have your special adult share it with you.

The Magical Ship

As you let yourself become comfortable and relaxed, imagine that it's a warm summer evening. The sun is low in the sky, and its golden rays fall softly on you as you lie on a comfortable cushion on a beautiful sailboat. Off in the distance, you see a beautiful island with a grassy meadow. You are feeling safe, warm, and comfortable as your boat takes you to the shore of the island. Everything seems to shine with a magical golden light. As you approach the shore, you hear a cute barking sound. Looking out over the side of your boat, you see a seal with friendly eyes and a kind face. He has a bag for you. In the bag, you find the sweetest apples. You get off the boat and step onto the island. You feel the soft, warm sand in between your toes, and you begin walking down a lovely path that has beautiful, tall grass on either side. You take a bite of an apple and taste how juicy, sweet, and crisp it is. You see a patch of soft grass that feels as soft as the coziest blanket you've ever felt. You lie down in the grass, and your eyes feel heavy and warm. You close your eyes and dream of magical unicorns who will take care of you as you sleep. You are feeling so happy, loved, safe, and warm as you drift off to a peaceful and restful sleep. Good night.

RESILIENCE CHECKPOINT

Way to go! We hope that you've grown your resilient behaviors by *doing* the activities in this section. Keep practicing them to make them stick.

Here is a quick summary of what you have learned:

- To build your "I can do it" muscles by developing confidence, control, and competence
- To be brave and practice hard things
- Coping skills that work for you
- To problem solve like a pro and be flexible like a sail
- To use and grow your strengths and superpowers
- Self-care activities that work for you

Check your learning a little more with a fun quiz.

1. Cross out the "C" word that doesn't build the "I can do it" muscles.

Confidence Control Competence Careful

2. Being brave means not being afraid. T or F

3. Unscramble these coping skills.

kate a pdee rbaeht ktal htiw a puwnrog teirw wndo uroy seelfing

4. Fill in the blank.

A sail and rope are ______________________________.

An anchor is ______________________________.

5. My superpower strength is: ______________________________
(There is no right answer; it can be anything you choose.)

6. Self-care means you are being selfish. T or F

Answers: 1. Careful. 2. False. 3. Take a deep breath. Talk with a grown-up. Write down your feelings. 4. Flexible, inflexible. 5. Whatever you wrote down is great! 6. F

WORD SUDOKU

Place a letter in each empty box so that every row, column, and nine-box square contains each of the letters featured in the grid. All the possible letters are in the grid. The last row of the grid will spell out an important message. (And the answers, if you need them at any point, are in the Answer Key at the very end of the book.)

						A		
G			N	M	I			
			T		S			I
S	M							R
		N	M					
A	I			G	O	S		
	N					I		A
								T
I			S				N	G

When Rebecca and Caren tried to solve this one, it required patience, hard work, and learning from our errors. Did that happen to you? If it did, that's DOING resilience. Great job!

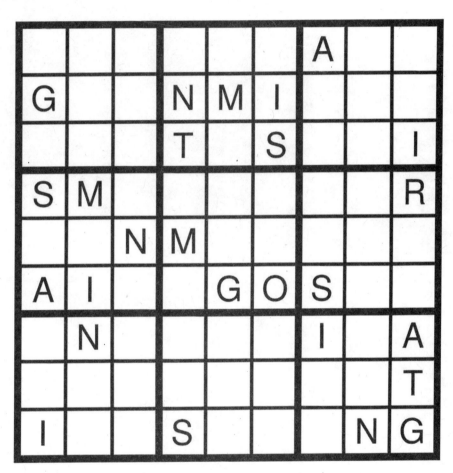

PART 5

Building Resilience All Around You

It takes a village to raise a child. Find a village. Encourage one another and open your village to one another.

—Proverb

What You'll Discover

Ta-da! You made it to the last part of the book! We are so proud of you. Up until now, you have grown your resilience by focusing on changing yourself—your emotions, thoughts, and behaviors. However, resilience does not exist only in you. Your culture, surroundings, and setting play an essential role in building your resilience. So it's equally important to grow resilience by gaining support from others.

In part 5, you will:

- Learn the importance of building connections and gaining support
- Find out how to connect to a larger supportive community
- Engage in giving and helping others
- Find a sense of meaning and purpose

ACTIVITY 28

Making Connections

LEARN IT

The research is clear: to build resilience, you need to feel connected to friends, family, and your community. Research shows that having just one adult who believes in you and has your back can help you manage stress, overcome adversity (a big word that means "very difficult times"), and build resilience.

Relationships are important because they help you feel less alone. Having a trusted person in your life can help you make sense of the challenges you are facing. That special person can give you a hug, validate your feelings, and help you figure out how to move forward in healthy and meaningful ways. In addition, having good relationships makes you feel happier and more confident—all building blocks of resilience.

Sometimes when we're feeling challenged or going through a hard time, our natural reaction is to isolate from others, as though we are a turtle hiding inside our shell. Or we may feel angry like a porcupine and use our spikes to push people away. However, by acting in these ways, we will end up more isolated and ultimately more stressed.

If you tend to react in these ways, try to do the opposite. That is, if you're feeling like a turtle, it's okay to take a few moments in your shell, and then do the opposite and reach out to someone to share how you're feeling. If you are feeling like a porcupine, you can do the opposite by trying to be more open, accepting help from people if they offer it to you.

DO IT

Who are the people you can reach out to for support? Write their names in the table below.

Place	Names
At home:	
At school:	

STRENGTHEN IT

It's easy to forget who your support people are when you're feeling stressed. Create a card to remind yourself that you are never alone. Cut it out and carry it with you wherever you go.

When I am feeling stressed or overwhelmed, I can reach out to:

____

____

Give yourself a hug and remind yourself:

- This is just a moment of time, and it will pass.
- Everyone goes through difficult times.
- I am not alone.

BONUS

(Do this one with your special adult.)

Draw a picture or take a photo of your support people. Share this picture with your special adult or the people in the picture. Notice how you and others feel after sharing.

ACTIVITY 29

Finding Your Community

LEARN IT

Knowing there's one person who has your back is great, but feeling like you're part of a larger community can develop your resilience even more. Schools, youth clubs, sports teams, and religious institutions are examples of ways you can connect with the wider community. When you're part of a community, you feel less alone during challenging times and gain a greater sense of security.

And you don't need to create a sense of community through only formal community connections. Informal community connections such as extended family, neighbors, mentors and teachers, youth groups, and friend groups are just as powerful, if not more powerful, in building resilience.

You may not find your community right away. Sometimes it takes a little work. Start by finding one person who shares your interests. Then, you might try to increase your group of two to a larger group who share similar interests. If you are still feeling stuck, find grown-ups to help you along the way. When you feel connected to the world around you, your confidence blossoms, and you can do better in school and feel more in control of your life.

DO IT

No one can steer a big boat all by themselves. You need a crew. In the last activity, you identified your support people at home and at school. For this exercise, fill the boat up with all the names of people in your larger community who make up your crew. This could include the neighbors, the Boys & Girls Club, or your pastor or rabbi— whoever you want to be part of your "boat community."

STRENGTHEN IT

Getting involved in a community service project is a great way to build a sense of community while doing something good for others. It can be something at school, like providing recycling bins, or it could benefit the larger community, like helping prepare food at a shelter.

My community service project is: ______________________________

When you do the project, do some journaling here about how it went.

How did it go?

____

____

Did you feel more connected to the people you worked with? And the people you helped?

____

____

Would you want to do more community service in the future? What would you like to do and where?

____

____

ACTIVITY 30

Helping Others

LEARN IT

In the last activity, we talked about the importance of community service. How do you usually feel after you help others? If you're like most, you noticed that when you support others, not only does the other person benefit, but you do too!

Helping others can have the same positive impact on your brain as receiving a present or eating your favorite food. Scientists have even discovered that being kind to others improves your happiness more than shopping or watching TV.

Giving back to others helps you take your mind off your own problems. When you focus on someone else, your own problems seem smaller and your outlook gets broader. Also, helping others makes it easier for you to ask for help when you need it. Once you experience how good it feels to be a helper, it's easier to ask for help. Being willing to ask for help is a necessary step to overcoming challenges.

DO IT

Let's play the kindness bingo game. Try to complete *five* kind activities in one day. Then, see if you can finish the whole board in one week.

Let someone go ahead of you in line.	Donate money to your favorite charity.	Help set or clear the table.	Say thank you to a classmate.
Say hi to the neighbor.	Pick up an item that fell.	Reach out to a friend.	Give your parent(s) a hug.
Open the door for someone.	Do something unexpected for someone in your family.	Take out the garbage.	Compliment someone today.
Invite someone to join your game.	Pick up trash or recycle.	Water the plants or feed an animal.	Actively listen when a friend talks to you.
Say hello and goodbye to your teacher.	Call a relative you haven't spoken to in a long time.	Write a letter to someone at school thanking them.	Give a friend or family member a simple gift.

STRENGTHEN IT

Put your strengths or superpowers to work. Use one of your top strengths you identified in activity 26 (see the list below) to help others. When you use your strengths for *kindness*, you benefit as well as the people you are supporting.

Strengths:

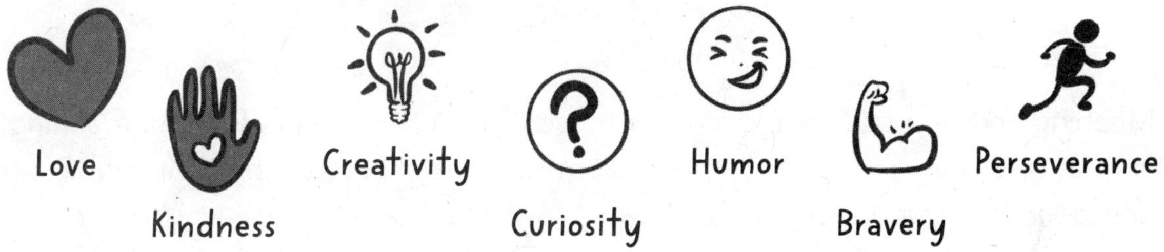

One of my strengths is: ____

I can use my strength to help others by: ________________________________

____

____

____

ACTIVITY 31

Developing Meaning and Purpose

LEARN IT

Meaning and purpose are big ideas, but we'll break them down for you. *Meaning* is what gives your life value. *Purpose* is having goals that are important to you and benefit the world too.

When people can find meaning in their lives, they can find the strength to overcome tough and even painful things. This isn't to say that pain isn't real. Rather, it's that meaning and purpose allow you to see that you're suffering *and* (remember your "and" skills from activity 18) that there's still hope and purpose in life.

When you act in ways that reflect your meaning and your purpose, it produces positive emotions, which leads to improved coping and greater resilience.

Again, this is big stuff. But it's still worth thinking about.

In activity 19, we discussed what was important to you, or your values. Go back to that activity and review what you selected. For example, if family is a value for you, choosing actions that make your family a priority will give you a sense of meaning and purpose. Let's say you're stressed-out and sad about remote school during COVID. When your mom asks how your day was, you take out your frustration by yelling at her. But if you remember your value of family—

something that gives your life meaning—you may choose to calm down so you don't hurt her feelings.

For some families, spirituality or religion give them a sense of meaning and purpose. Religions connect people in a community, making the whole group as important as each person. But you don't need to be religious to have a sense of purpose. Values like kindness, teamwork, and giving, which are bigger than you, are also good places to find meaning and purpose, especially during difficult or really stressful times.

Now, we want to share something that's pretty incredible. It's possible that out of a terrible event, a positive change can occur.

Let's say you've lived through a wildfire that destroyed your home. There's no doubt this would be very painful. But you might find meaning in your family surviving. You could be touched by all the neighbors who helped out. And you might decide that it's part of your purpose to help other kids who go through wildfires in the future to feel safer and stronger. You could decide to learn about climate change and get involved in local politics when you get older. This is something called *post-traumatic growth*.

In post-traumatic growth, people who have been through a lot of stress and really tough things develop new ways to see themselves and the world they live in. They recognize how difficult it was to go through what they went through. They also learn that they are strong and that some good can come out of a painful experience. And their lives don't get defined by their hardships. Instead, they focus on their strengths, their values, and their desire for a meaningful life.

You can learn to respond in these brave ways too, no matter what life brings you.

DO IT

To help you find more meaning and purpose, explore the following questions about a challenge or stressor you had to face or are facing now.

- Has anything positive come from dealing with this problem?
- How can this situation prepare you for a future challenge?
- How can others benefit and learn from what you went through?

STRENGTHEN IT

Ask yourself a series of *why* questions to help you discover your sense of meaning and purpose. To get started, think about something you do. For example, *I go to school*. Then ask yourself, *Why*? Once you have an answer, question the answer by asking *why* again. Ask why at least three to four times to get to the true meaning or purpose for what you do.

See how Mina completed this activity below.

Why do you go to school?

↓

Answer: To learn.

Why do you need to learn?

↓

Answer: So I can get a job.

Why do you need a job?

↓

Answer: So I can support my family and have a good life. (This is what gives Mina's life meaning and purpose.)

Your turn.

Why...?

↓

Answer: ______________________

Why...?

↓

Answer: ______________________

Why...?

↓

Answer: ______________________

Why...?

↓

Answer: ______________________

BONUS

(Do this one with your special adult.)

Did you discover your *why*? Share it with your special adult. To make sure you don't forget your *why*, draw a picture of your *why* below. Keep that picture front and center. And use your *why* as your North Star, helping you steer your ship even when there are no other landmarks in sight.

ACTIVITY 32

Putting It All Together

LEARN IT

Remember at the beginning of this book we discussed how life can be stormy? We asked you to imagine yourself on a boat in the middle of a big storm. The boat was swaying wildly, the waves were crashing, land was nowhere in sight, and there was no North Star to guide you.

Then you imagined that you were on this same boat, but this time, you were with an experienced captain, and you had strong swimming skills, a life jacket, a solid anchor, GPS, and a North Star to guide you. We asked you if you would do better in the storm with all that support. Remember?

Our hope is that by completing the activities in the workbook, you feel that you're on a more stable, well-supported ship, one that's fully equipped with everything you'll need and moving toward safer waters.

We hope that you'll continue to use the STORMS approach when navigating life's ups and downs. And remember, STORMS stands for:

S. Starts with adult resilience. When adults grow their own resilience, they can better help themselves and you.

T. Teach yourself the skills and science of resilience.

O. Own all your emotions, so they don't control you. Feel your feelings, even the hard ones.

R. Rule your mind so you can think happier and more helpful thoughts.

M. Manage your behaviors so you can cope more and stress less.

S. Seek a support network (parent, teacher, friend, neighbor) so you'll always have someone there to help you, even when things are hard.

DO IT

Look back at the survey you took in activity 2 one more time to see how much your resilience has grown. Answer the questions again, in a different color ink. Did you grow in the areas where you gave yourself a thumbs-sideways or thumbs-down before? Do you have more thumbs-ups?

Whatever results you got, give yourself a pat on the back for all the work you've done. Building resilience is a lifelong project. It takes time. But by working through the activities in this book, you have taken steps to creating a better world for yourself—and for all of us. A world where we all feel strong, courageous, able to face whatever comes our way, and in a word, "resilient."

STRENGTHEN IT

As you have discovered, when you help others, you also help yourself. Keeping this in mind, imagine that you have a friend or relative who is struggling to be resilient. Then, write a letter to this person, sharing the STORMS approach to help that person build resilience. We have provided a fill-in-the-blanks format to help you write this letter. Writing this letter will help another, as well as you.

Dear ________________________,

As you know, I had the challenge of ____.

(Describe a challenge you've experienced here.)

I hope that by sharing how I was able to grow from this experience, you will be able to better face your challenge and become stronger from it. I know you've been struggling with ____.

(Describe your friend's challenge here.)

What helped me first was that the grown-ups grew their own resilience so they could help themselves and me. Here's how my grown-ups helped:

____.

(Describe the S: Starts with adult resilience. How did your adults grow their own resilience?)

Next, I learned all about what it means to be resilient and how some stress can be helpful, but too much stress is not: ________________________________

____

(Describe the T: Something you taught yourself about resilience.)

Then, I tried my best to accept all my feelings by: ________________________

____.

(Describe the O: How you owned your emotions, especially the yucky ones.)

I got better at catching, checking, and challenging unhelpful thoughts and replacing them with more helpful ways of thinking. Here are some ways I did that:

____.

(Describe the R: How you challenged unhelpful thoughts and developed helpful ones.)

When I felt overwhelmed, I used coping strategies such as: ______________________

____.

(Describe the M: How you managed your behavior to cope better and stress less.)

Lastly, I made sure I had my people. I talked to: ______________________________.

(Describe the S: A person who gives you support.)

I also spent time with ____ and went

(Describe friends you spend time with.)

to ____.

(Describe a place you go when you need support).

Maybe you could come with me or you could join:

____

(Describe a community activity they could join.)

I now know that I can take on hard things in the future and you can too. I grew from this challenge, and I can tell because ________________________________

____.

(Describe how you grew from the challenge.)

Love always,

Your bestie

____

(Your name.)

Read through everything you just wrote. The letter you wrote is awesome, and so are you!

If you just don't want this book to end, check out a few bonus activities on self-compassion, mindfulness, and more that we have included online at http//newharbinger.com/49166. (If you need help finding them, talk to your special adult.)

RESILIENCE CHECKPOINT

You did it! You made it to the last checkpoint. Be sure to celebrate all you have learned and accomplished. Here is a quick summary of what we hope you learned in part 5:

- That resilience isn't only on you: your environment matters
- The importance of building connections with other people and the larger community
- Ways to give to and help others
- How to create meaning and a sense of purpose in your life

For this last resilience checkpoint, we will ask you about material covered in part 5 and the rest of the book. Feel free to go back to look for the answers if you need to. You know what we are going to say at this point: that's being resilient.

TRUE OR FALSE?

1. Resilience is the ability to cope with life's ups and downs and grow from challenges.	TRUE	FALSE
2. Most people will not have to face challenges in their lives.	TRUE	FALSE
3. Stress is always bad.	TRUE	FALSE
4. All feelings, even the yucky ones, are beneficial.	TRUE	FALSE
5. The situation, and not your thoughts, affects how you feel.	TRUE	FALSE
6. Self-efficacy is built when you do hard things and master them.	TRUE	FALSE
7. When you can find some meaning in what has happened to you, you can experience post-traumatic growth.	TRUE	FALSE
8. You are awesome for completing all the activities.	TRUE	FALSE

ANSWER KEY FOR TRUE AND FALSE

1. **True!** Resilience is the ability to cope with life's ups and downs and grow from challenges.

2. **False!** No one gets a free ride in the game of life.

3. **False!** There is helpful stress, workable stress, and unhelpful stress. The good news is that working through these stresses can grow you as a person.

4. **True!** Yucky feelings help by signaling that something bad is going on and preparing you for a true crisis.

5. **False!** It is your *thoughts*, not the situation, that affect how you feel and act.

6. **True!** Self-efficacy is believing in your ability to solve a problem or perform a task. Self-efficacy is built when you do hard things and master them.

7. **True!** Connecting to your sense of meaning can help you experience post-traumatic growth and grow as a person.

8. **Very True!** You, our dear reader, were awesome before and you are even more awesome now!

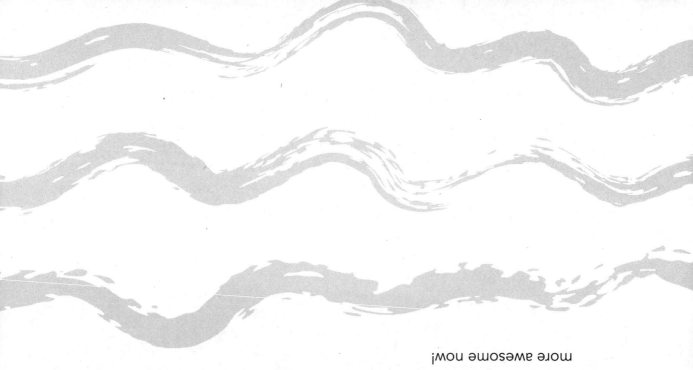

THE LIGHTHOUSE PUZZLE

A lighthouse guides you safely to shore the same way this puzzle will guide you to the final message of this book. Return to the puzzles at the end of each of the previous parts of the book to fill in the gaps in these four words. Then transfer the letters into the numbered spaces in the lighthouse grid.

Part 1. O ___ T I ___ I ___ T I ___
 1 2 3 4

Part 2. E M ___ T I O ___ S
 5 6

Part 3. M ___ N ___ S ___ T
 7 8 9

Part 4. S ___ ___ O N G
 10 11

Now use the clues that are listed to fill out the rest of the squares. Note: Some rows contain two separate words, as indicated by an asterisk (*). When they're filled out correctly, the shaded spaces on each side of the lighthouse reading downward will spell out the message of this book.

CLUES:
Baseball stat
Prepare to be published
Slow creature
Squid's squirt * Glide down a slope
Camper's light
Frozen water * Cube
Mistake * Super small
Not once * Hogwarts subject
Common cafeteria food
Dumbo * Pinto or kidney

7
8
3 10
6 3
6 10 11
7 5 4
11 5 2 7
6 9 7 4
9 3 7
9 1 10 9 6

We are so proud of you and all your hard work. You've done so many activities and learned so many skills in this book: how to handle tough thoughts and feelings, how to trust yourself and use your strengths when you encounter challenges, and how to build your connections with the people you love and enjoy life. If you continue to practice the skills you've learned, you'll continue to grow, learn, and build your resilience. We believe in you!

Your captains,

—Caren and Rebecca

Acknowledgments

This workbook would not be possible without the help of many. A tremendous thank you to Dr. Robert Brooks for your support for this project. Whenever we were stuck and in need of a "charismatic adult," we could always count on you.

Thank you to our family, friends, and colleagues who listened, read, and provided feedback. We could not have completed this workbook without your guidance and support.

Thank you to the staff at New Harbinger Publications—acquisitions editor Elizabeth Hollis Hansen and senior editor Vicraj Gill—as well as to copyeditor Gretel Hakanson for all your edits, feedback, and more edits. We think we made a workbook that was better because of it. A special thank-you to Daisy Florin. Your ability to edit and question our thinking is reflected in the workbook. Thank you, Debbie Manber Kupfer of Paws 4 Puzzles, for the amazing puzzles. The puzzles provide a great way to practice those resilient skills. And thank you to Valeria Chipao for the illustrations throughout the book.

Finally, we are grateful to you, the reader, and your special adult, for taking this journey with us and for giving us the opportunity to write this book. By giving to you, we gave to ourselves. The process has made us both more optimistic, braver, purposeful, and resilient.

Answer Key

RESILIENCE CHECKPOINT 1: OUR UNSINKABLE BOAT

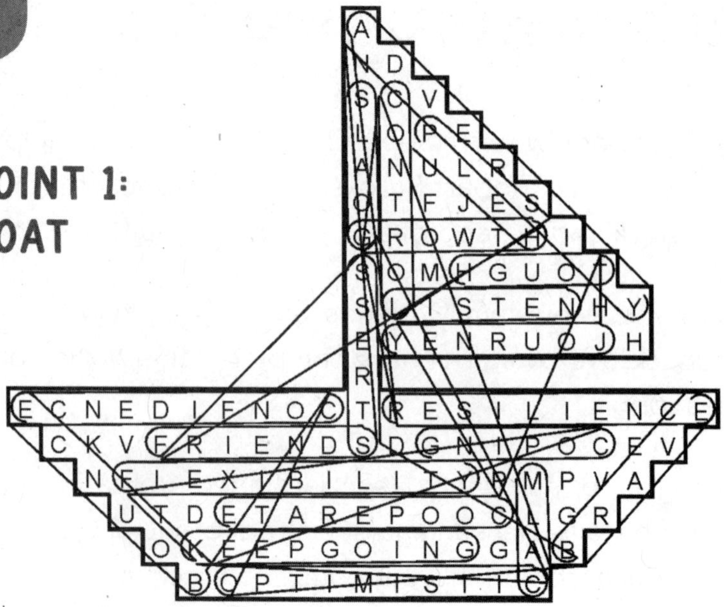

ACTIVITY 11: STAYING PRESENT AND MINDFUL: BONUS

Breathe in, smile, and touch your heart.

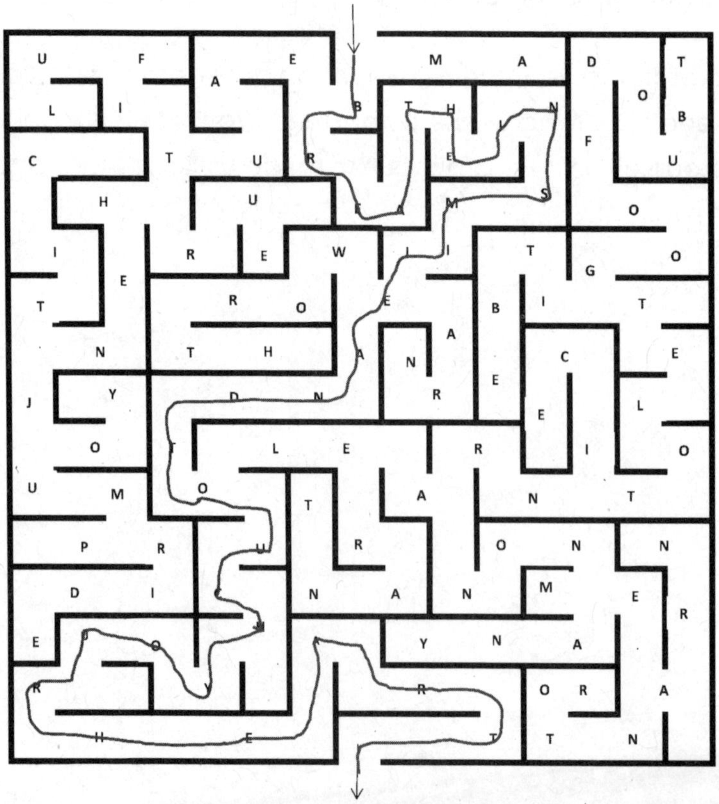

RESILIENCE CHECKPOINT 3: CROSSWORD PUZZLE

							1 A			2 P		3 Y		
4 F	A	C	T		5 M	U	S	C	L	E		E		6 F
E				7 W			K			8 S	U	S	H	I
E		9 S	A	I	L		S			S				X
L		E		S				10 D	O	I	N	11 G		E
12 I	R	E		13 H	O	P	14 E			M		15 R	I	D
N							V			I		A		M
16 G	R	17 O	W	18 T	H	M	I	N	D	S	E	T		I
		P		R			D			M		I		N
19 Y	E	T		20 A	B	L	E					T		D
U		21 I	M	P			N		22 V	A	L	U	E	S
R		M					C		I			D		E
23 T	H	I	N	K		24 P	E	R	M	25 A	N	E	26 N	T
		S								N			E	
27 T	I	M	E		28 S	H	O	U	L	D		29 A	T	E

RESILIENCE CHECKPOINT 4: WORD SUDOKU

I am strong.

N	S	I	O	R	G	A	T	M
G	T	A	N	M	I	R	O	S
M	O	R	T	A	S	N	G	I
S	M	O	I	N	T	G	A	R
R	G	N	M	S	A	T	I	O
A	I	T	R	G	O	S	M	N
T	N	S	G	O	M	I	R	A
O	R	G	A	I	N	M	S	T
I	A	M	S	T	R	O	N	G

RESILIENCE CHECKPOINT 5: THE LIGHTHOUSE PUZZLE

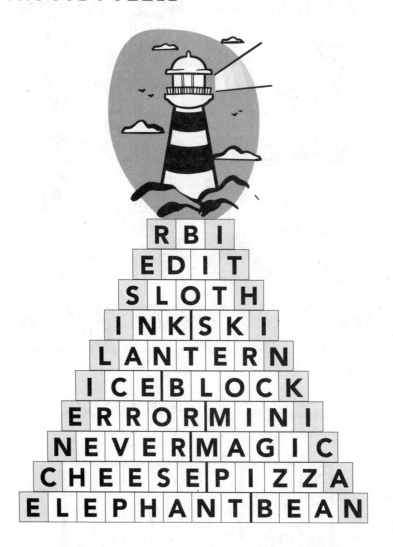

RBI

EDIT

SLOTH

INKSKI

LANTERN

ICEBLOCK

ERRORMINI

NEVERMAGIC

CHEESEPIZZA

ELEPHANTBEAN

Caren Baruch-Feldman, PhD, is a clinical psychologist and a certified school psychologist. She maintains a private practice in Scarsdale, NY; and works as a school psychologist in Harrison, NY. She is also author of *The Grit Guide for Teens*. Baruch-Feldman has authored numerous articles and led workshops on topics such as cognitive behavioral therapy (CBT) techniques, helping children and adults cope with stress and worry, helping people change, and developing grit and self-control. She is a fellow and supervisor in rational emotive behavior therapy (REBT), a type of CBT. Visit her online at www.drbaruchfeldman.com.

Rebecca Comizio, MA, MEd, was named Connecticut's 2019 School Psychologist of the Year. She is a practicing school psychologist, and licensed professional counselor at the New Canaan Country School in New Canaan, CT; and the Waverly Group in Old Greenwich, CT. Comizio is founder and cohost of the *School Psyched Podcast*. She also serves in leadership roles for the National Association of School Psychologists (NASP). Comizio is coauthor of *70 Play Activities for Better Thinking, Self-Regulation, Learning, and Behavior.*

Foreword writer **Robert Brooks, PhD**, is coauthor of *Raising Resilient Children* and *The Power of Resilience*.

MORE BOOKS from NEW HARBINGER PUBLICATIONS

DON'T LET YOUR EMOTIONS RUN YOUR LIFE FOR KIDS

A DBT-Based Skills Workbook to Help Children Manage Mood Swings, Control Angry Outbursts, and Get Along with Others

978-1626258594 / US $18.95

Instant Help Books
An Imprint of New Harbinger Publications

THE GRIT WORKBOOK FOR KIDS

CBT Skills to Help Kids Cultivate a Growth Mindset and Build Resilience

978-1684035984 / US $16.95

Instant Help Books
An Imprint of New Harbinger Publications

MASTER OF MINDFULNESS

How to Be Your Own Superhero in Times of Stress

978-1626254640 / US $14.95

Instant Help Books
An Imprint of New Harbinger Publications

THE RESILIENCE RECIPE

A Parent's Guide to Raising Fearless Kids in the Age of Anxiety

978-1684036967 / US $18.95

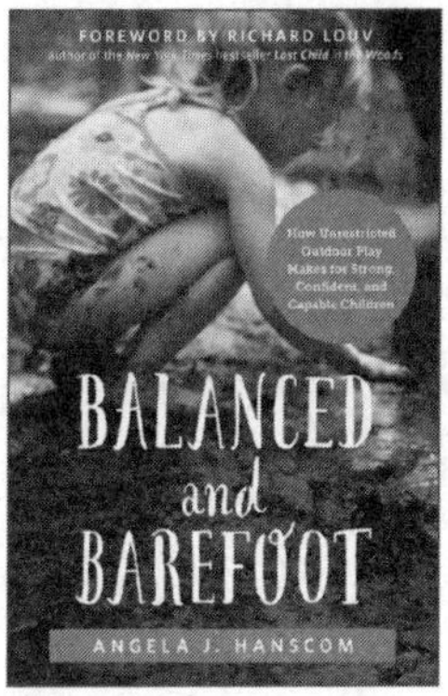

BALANCED AND BAREFOOT

How Unrestricted Outdoor Play Makes for Strong, Confident, and Capable Children

978-1626253735 / US $17.95

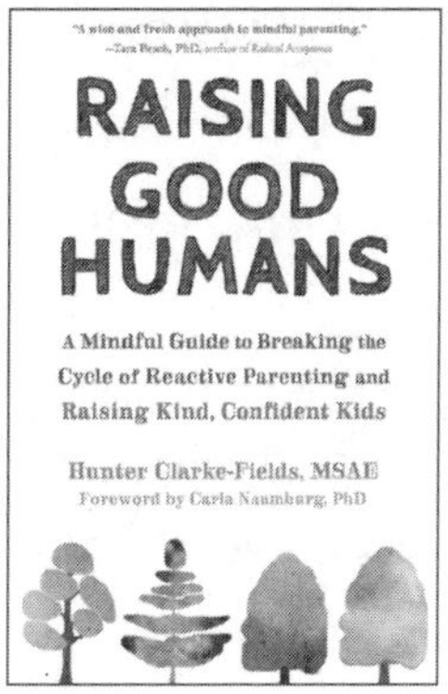

RAISING GOOD HUMANS

A Mindful Guide to Breaking the Cycle of Reactive Parenting and Raising Kind, Confident Kids

978-1684033881 / US $16.95

new**harbinger**publications

1-800-748-6273 / newharbinger.com

(VISA, MC, AMEX / prices subject to change without notice)

Follow Us

Don't miss out on new books from New Harbinger.
Subscribe to our email list at **newharbinger.com/subscribe**

Did you know there are **free tools** you can download for this book?

Free tools are things like **worksheets, guided meditation exercises**, and **more** that will help you get the most out of your book.

You can download free tools for this book—whether you bought or borrowed it, in any format, from any source—from the New Harbinger website. All you need is a NewHarbinger.com account. Just use the URL provided in this book to view the free tools that are available for it. Then, click on the "download" button for the free tool you want, and follow the prompts that appear to log in to your NewHarbinger.com account and download the material.

You can also save the free tools for this book to your **Free Tools Library** so you can access them again anytime, just by logging in to your account! Just look for this button on the book's free tools page.

+ Save this to my free tools library

If you need help accessing or downloading free tools, visit **newharbinger.com/faq** or contact us at **customerservice@newharbinger.com.**